T0329190

Financing Africa

Attiya Waris

Langaa Research & Publishing CIG
Mankon, Bamenda

Publisher:
Langaa RPCIG
Langaa Research & Publishing Common Initiative Group
P.O. Box 902 Mankon
Bamenda
North West Region
Cameroon
Langaagrp@gmail.com
www.langaa-rpcig.net

Distributed in and outside N. America by African Books Collective
orders@africanbookscollective.com
www.africanbookscollective.com

ISBN-10: 9956-551-49-x
ISBN-13: 978-9956-551-49-1

Reference as:
Waris, A. *Financing Africa*. Bamenda: Langaa.

Praise for the Book

"Professor Waris' work on fiscal and tax issues in Africa is a serious and helpful contribution. The subject is complex, but the book succeeds in presenting a clear, readable and interesting analysis."

Mohammed "Mo" Ibrahim,
Founder, Mo Ibrahim Foundation

"As a reporter, I regularly dig into tax avoidance issues and illicit financial flows. Professor Waris' clearheaded insights are a boon. We nonexperts can no longer say, 'It's all too complicated' or 'I don't know where to start.' This book provides resources for journalists to help keep issues of public interest on the front page."

Will Fitzgibbon,
International Consortium of Investigative Journalists

"This is an incredibly important book from one of the leading authors on Africa and taxation. Supported by a granular and insightful analysis of Africa's 54 countries, this book is required reading for all those interested in taxation and sustainability. This is an exciting contribution, and strongly recommended."

Prof. Ann Mumford,
Dickson Poon School of Law, King's College London

"This is *the* book to read to understand fiscal systems and development. It canvasses the entire African continent. Waris has combined economic data and law to make taxation and its impact on socioeconomic development understandable. Poorly designed tax policy has poor outcomes on tax revenues, results in market distortions, and drives consumption behaviors toward undesirable paths. Thorough analysis such as in this book should inform tax policy design, choice of tax instruments, and rate adjustments."

Prof. Njuguna N'dungu, Executive
Director, African Economic Research Consortium

"Drawing upon her wide knowledge of law, philosophy, and history, as well as the data resources of the University of Nairobi, Attiya Waris provides a carefully explained and extensively illustrated examination of fiscal and tax issues confronting Africa. This important work thoroughly frames policy options and opportunities available to elected officials and administrators moving forward the economic and political wellbeing of the continent. Essential reading."

Raymond Baker, Founding
President, Global Financial Integrity

"*Financing Africa* unpacks the continent and explores the nexus between the management of fiscal policy and good governance. It lends insight into terms people consider technical and incomprehensible and uses real and contextualized examples. It will allow Africans to not only better understand each other but also to better interact and build their financial relationships."

Akere Muna, Member, High Level
Panel on Illicit Financial Flows from Africa

"A unique and valuable contribution to the commonwealth of learning on tax in Africa. Waris lucidly explains how the fiscal needs of governments are linked with fairness, administrability and economic growth in contemporary African tax systems. She draws on historical and interdisciplinary approaches to highlight the need for legitimacy, the rule of law and taxpayer rights to achieve tax compliance and effective collection."

Miranda Stewart, Professor
of Law, University of Melbourne

"In a continent constantly seeking to redefine her global standing, especially on the edge of Development Economics, Professor Waris bursts through with the reflective freshness and futuristic analysis that unmasks the complexities of the web of fiscal and tax laws in Africa, simplifying them to become useful tools for budget reform and social justice. Her comparative scrutiny of African fiscal systems and legal frameworks judiciously questions gaps in gender data and thus engenders discourse on opportunities for women within Africa's taxation laws. Her analysis includes aspirational and profound citations and insights from African cultures. It will help us chart Africa's future taxation path and, by extension, reduce inequalities across the continent. Her book is indeed a thinking mechanism that Africa desperately needs."

Memory Kachambwa, Executive Director, African Women's Development and Communication Network (FEMNET)

"*Financing Africa* examines the financial systems of different African countries and identifies systems, ideas and practices that promote the goals of the state while securing public participation and the rights of citizens to information. This continental perspective, which infuses eloquence and wit into highly technical subject matters and provides new insights into financing Africa's development, is accessible to both experts and laypersons. Professor Waris shows the way forward for African integration, from a fiscal perspective. She adopts a people-centric approach to discourse on matters of taxation, reminding us all that the state is financed by the sweat of the brow of the citizenry, and, as such, governments should ensure that this limited resource is always prudently utilized. This thought-provoking read will undoubtedly be a staple point of reference in all discussions on financing Africa's development."

Joseph K. Kinyua, Head of the Public Service of Kenya

"Many African and non-African international governmental and non-governmental organisations have shown interest in the development of tax policies in Africa, and Professor Attiya Waris in this book applies a series of principles, concepts and considerations that enable the reader to form a balanced view on the development of tax policies in Africa and to understand that there is much more to study, and much more to do."

Jos Beerepoot, Global Tax Director, ABN AMRO Bank

Dedication

For

All My People

the

People of the World

and

to their striving

individually and collectively

for

better living standards

for

ALL

Acknowledgements

The support from people across the world and of all ages, some of whom have now passed, has been inspiring. It has been a true joy to work with people who struggle to better understand the world in which we live. This book would never have been possible without the incredible teachers through whose hands I have passed. Also, my patient and kind parents allowed me space to focus on it.

My inspirations: Khalajaan Noori, the most memorable influence outside of my parents, and Prof. Sol Picciotto, who continues to inspire and support my development as a researcher and teacher. Several professors have supported me on my journey: Len Seabrook, Ann Mumford, Kathleen Lahey, Gorik Ooms. So has my sister Annet Oguttu.

My tribe: Lyla who challenges me. Milhia who encourages me to reach farther. Sameena who calms me, Sharon who checks on me (and, when need be, keeps me in check), and Maureen who always makes me laugh. Shabnam who celebrates with me and Shazeela who has my back!

My colleagues, researchers and students: fellow teachers, researchers and students at the University of Nairobi, at KU Leuven, in Pretoria, and in Rwanda. Lecturers and researchers heard my ideas, pulled them apart, and encouraged me to continue this difficult journey. My wonderful students provided incisive feedback. Thank you!

My team at the Committee on Fiscal Studies at the University of Nairobi: Bosire, Mary, Manuela, Bena, Mokeira, Stella, Nick, Dick, Jack, Maina, Elvis, Everlyn, Michelle, Moses, Vallarrie, Andrew, Joan, Waridah, Lesikel, Warren and Rushda. I have learnt a lot from you all and your energy. Your hunger for knowledge continues to inspire my research.

My reviewers and editors: This journey to publication and the struggle to find an African publisher proved challenging. I cannot thank the Langaa team enough for making a difficult journey end so pleasantly.

There are many others: those in international organizations like the UN, OECD, IMF, WB, AU, and ATAF; numerous researchers and finance and development-related ministry staff; revenue commissioners and their staff; and students across the world. They all willingly helped me access incredible data, some of which, in addition to featuring in this book, is for the first time publicly available online, from the University of Nairobi web site.

I am humbled by your support and faith in me and cannot thank you all enough.

Table of Contents

Appendices

List of Tables and Figures

Tables
1. Expected African state budget framework based on continental commitments
2. Major investments in Africa, in 2016
3. Taxpayers registered as a percentage of registered voters
4. Number of foreign corporations in (9) African countries
5. Budget expenditure breakdown of Guinea
6. Number of double tax agreements (DTAs) in African countries

Figures
1. Map of African countries with participatory budget processes
2. Map of African countries with freedom of information laws
3. GDP growth by region on the African continent
4. Share of African GDP growth by region
5. Taxpayers registered as a percentage of registered voters, in selected African countries as of December 2018
6. Mapping of taxpayer registration as a percent of registered voters, as of December 2018
7. Graph of number of foreign corporations in (9) African countries
8. Mapping of number of foreign corporations in (9) African countries
9. Percentage of GDP used on health spending
10. Mapping of percentage of GDP used on health pending
11. Images from Guinea's citizen guides on the national budget

Acronyms

AAAA	Addis Ababa Action Agenda
ACHPR	African Charter of Human and People's Rights
ACPCC	African Convention on Preventing and Combatting Corruption
ACS	African Charter on Statistics
ACVPDLGLD	African Charter on the Values and Principles of Decentralisation, Local Governance and Local Development
ACVPPSA	African Charter on the Values and Principles of Public Service and Administration
AfDB	African Development Bank
ADHS	Abuja Declaration on health spending
AfCFTA	African Continental Free Trade Agreement / Area
AFRITAC	African Regional Technical Assistance Center (of IMF)
ATAF	African Tax Administration Forum
ATI	Addis Tax Initiative
AU	African Union
BIA	Bilateral Investment Agreement
BIT	Bilateral Investment Treaty
BRICS	Brazil, Russia, India, China and South Africa
CGT	Capital Gains Tax
CIAT	Inter-American Center of Tax Administrations
CIT	Corporate Income Tax
COMESA	Common Market for Eastern and Southern Africa
DRC	Democratic Republic of Congo
DTA	Double Taxation Agreement
EAC	East African Community
EPZ	Export Processing Zone
FDI	Foreign Direct Investment
FfD	Financing for Development
FSI	Financial Secrecy Index
GDP	Gross Domestic Product
HIPC	Highly Indebted Poor Country
HL	House of Lords
HLTF	High Level Taskforce

ICIJ	International Consortium of Investigative Journalists
ICT	Information and Communication Technology
IFF	Illicit Financial Flows
IMF	International Monetary Fund
MDAFS	Maputo Declaration on Agriculture and Food Security
MDGs	Millennium Development Goals
MLI	Multilateral Instrument
MNC	Multinational Corporation
MNE	Multinational Enterprise
NEPAD	New Partnership for Africa's Development
NIFC	Nairobi International Financial Centre
OECD	Organisation for Economic Corporation and Development
PIT	Personal Income Tax
R&D	Research and Development
SACU	Southern African Customs Union
SADC	Southern African Development Community
SDGs	Sustainable Development Goals
SEZ	Special Economic Zone
SOE	State-Owned Enterprise
T	Target(s) of the SDGs
TC	Tax Court
TRA	Tanzania Revenue Authority
UAE	Unites Arab Emirates
UK	United Kingdom
UN	United Nations
UNCTAD	United Nations Conference on Trade and Development
UNDESA	United Nations Department of Economic and Social Affairs
UNECA	United Nations Economic Commission for Africa
US/USA	United States / United States of America
USD	United States Dollar
VAT	Value-Added Tax

Foreword

Rain does not fall on one roof alone.

Proverb from Cameroon

Reading through Attiya's book reminded me of this famous Cameroonian proverb, about rain not falling on one roof alone. Through my half century long career, I have watched my continent move in fits and starts. Some countries are moving along, and some seem to be moving steadily in the wrong direction. Aware of situations threatening to pull apart the fabric of our nations, a sense of responsibility weighs on my soul. We as Africans must put our knowledge and experiences at the service of our peoples and get to the source of issues – the system. The rain is falling on all of us.

We need to design good governance systems. It is essential to make reforms so that the individual controlling the process is not also a player in it. In many countries of our continent, those who govern are almost completely oblivious to the basic tenets of conflict of interest. The effects of a lopsided system emerge often decades later, so we must take care to understand systems in changing and rebuilding them. If the playing field is not evened out, the continent and individual African countries risk being stuck in interminable and exclusive loops created for only part of us. People will only stand for this for so long.

Attiya's first book, *Tax and Development*, the first of its kind globally, unpacked connecting finance to development. This book, *Financing Africa*, is an even greater achievement. It unpacks the African continent. It lends insight into terms people consider technical and incomprehensible and uses real and contextualized examples. This is a handbook not only for legal professionals like me but also government officials, politicians, and journalists as well as the general public interested in understanding how countries are financed.

Financing Africa is a fascinating analysis that tabulates and charts out African financial systems. It could not have come at a better time. We just passed the African Continental Free Trade Agreement and are looking to break down barriers across the continent. West African countries, both Anglophone and Francophone, all members of the Economic Community of West African States (ECOWAS) and with a population of about 385 million people, are putting everything in place to have a single currency by 2020. The success of such a venture will depend largely on the fiscal component of any arrangements made. The monetary and fiscal policies of the countries concerned will have to be aligned.

I met Attiya Waris over five years ago and was immediately taken in by her thinking on the nexus between the management of fiscal policy and good governance. As she says, it is necessary for there to be a "regularly renegotiated fiscal social contract between a country's population and its government."

Fiscal policy in many African countries is treated as something that concerns the government only and its revenue. The scrutiny of parliamentary oversight in many cases is hardly felt. Parliamentarians will find this book edifying as they seek to ensure that they are capacitated to negotiate any fiscal policy on behalf of those who elected them. As the American author Robert Heinlein aptly put it, "There is no worse tyranny than to force a man to pay for what he does not want merely because you think it would be good for him."

Attiya has showcased a wealth of knowledge and understanding of African systems in this book. The time she has taken to come up with this masterpiece is more than justified. She has taken a practical approach to a subject hitherto considered intimidating to many a reader. This book will allow Africans to not only better understand each other but also to better interact and build their financial relationships.

Akere Muna
Member, High Level Panel on
Illicit Financial Flows from Africa

Foreword

Professor Attiya Waris is one of the leading thinkers and writers on matters of financing development and state building in developing countries. Her contributions to advancing conversations around the interplay between fiscal law and policy, on one hand, and the state's obligations towards poverty alleviation, human rights and the equitable distribution of the gains of development, on the other, has been immense.

This book, *Financing Africa*, advances those conversations by examining the financial systems of different African countries and identifying systems, ideas and practices that promote the goals of the state while securing public participation and the rights of citizens to information. This continental perspective, written in Professor Waris' signature style of infusing eloquence and wit into highly technical subject matters, delivers new insights into this immensely important topic of financing Africa's development in a manner accessible to both experts in the field and laypersons.

Reading through the text, I was stuck by how elegantly the case for African integration, through common fiscal approaches, had been made. While most other authors write about taxation from a purely abstract point of view, Professor Waris adopts a people-centric approach to discourse on matters of taxation, reminding us all that the state is financed by the sweat of the brow of the citizenry, and, as such, governments should ensure that this limited resource is always prudently utilized. This sets her works apart from others and makes them relevant to a broader audience.

This thought-provoking read will undoubtedly be a staple point of reference in all discussions on financing Africa's development.

Joseph K. Kinyua,
Elder of the Order of the Golden Heart
of Kenya and Head of the Public Service

Preface

After the 14-year journey of writing this book and developing its companion website, a poem almost wrote itself. I share it here.

When I reflect on the diversity and magnitude of Africa, its vast lands and rich heritage, its 54 countries, thousands of communities, and millions of people with their unique abilities and challenges, I am awed and honoured to be part of this ancient yet young and vibrant continent. We are constructing narratives to guide Africa forward, which responsibility is in our hands.

This book is my contribution to understanding people, their financial resources, and state management of financial and fiscal systems on the African continent. Visits were made to Egypt, Morocco, Senegal, Rwanda, Uganda, Tanzania, Zambia, South Africa, Ghana, Nigeria and the Seychelles. I faced the usual challenges of finding up-to-date information and data, which makes assessment a challenge. The result is that this book is not intended to be comprehensive but rather a step in helping to chart out the future of the continent. **Drums beat!**

Our strong oral heritage inspired me towards proverbs and sayings to provide African insights into finance and taxes, which some consider dry and technical topics. I collected proverbs and sayings from diverse sources including from conversations with people across the continent. I have woven the proverbs into this text in the same way we weave them into formal systems of our everyday lives. **Songs Echo!**

We need to ensure we are heard, and this requires recording in writing what we do, how, when, where, with whom, and why. This contributes to science and to learning about and adapting society and systems. In interacting with documents and people, I was able to use English, Kiswahili and French. It was a challenge being in settings where Arabic, Spanish or a local vernacular language predominated. In working with my students, I became aware of how difficult it is for people with disabilities to access certain types of text. In a spirit of inclusiveness, I am happy to know that, thanks to the latest technological platforms, this book will be available in audio as well as the written word. **Voices Carry!**

The African continent is moving towards unity. Ideas and rhythms are circulating. We hope the mapping out of systems in this book, with the companion website housed at the University of Nairobi, helps us courageously and intelligently lead and govern our nations and continent. **Dancers Vibrate!**

It is important to look not just at our strengths but also our weaknesses. What do we want to change? What can we improve? Let us not hide our weaknesses. This book looks at positive and negative results in unpacking the continent. **The Mist Hides!**

No matter what we do to our precious continent, it continues to cradle us. This book, it is hoped, will lend us a better understanding of our words and deeds and the effects they have not only on our continent but on the world. **The Earth Absorbs!**

It is my hope that this book gives readers a basic and nuanced understanding of the design of African financial systems. It also shows how legislation, regulations and policies are being creatively used to develop at sub-national, national, regional and continental levels. It is by no means a complete analysis of this vast continent but rather a snapshot of its rich diversity in the design of financial systems.

Any errors in the work are entirely my own, and I am fully aware of not only its weaknesses but some glaring gaps in information. I would be honoured and grateful to receive any information that can clarify or improve the work for future editions.

I am delighted to present this work with its companion website (see Appendix A) that houses the data I collected on my journey.

Drums Beat!
Songs Echo!
Voices Carry!
Dancers Vibrate!
The Mist Hides!
The Earth Absorbs!

Joy Rises to the Heavens!
The Heart is at Peace!

Introduction: Understanding Fiscal Law and Policy

You think of water when the well is empty.

Proverb from Ethiopia

By July 2019, 54 African countries had signed the African Continental Free Trade Agreement (AfCFTA), and the treaty has moved into the operational phase. The African Union under the stewardship of Rwanda and President Kagame, and diverse United Nations (UN) bodies including the United Nations Economic Commission for Africa (UNECA) and the United Nations Conference on Trade and Development (UNCTAD), pushed forward this agenda to change the fiscal landscape on the African continent.

Intra-African trade is approximately 5% of total African trade, and some say this treaty and its implementation will change the landscape, boosting intra-African trade by 60%.[1][2] Several initiatives preceded AfCFTA: the global UN-led Financing for Development (FfD) processes, the Millennium Development Goals[3] (MDGs), the Sustainable Development Goals[4] (SDGs), and the Addis Tax Initiative (ATI)[5]. In addition, data and debates on issues related to illicit financial flows[6], unpaid care work, the informal economy, the impact of digitisation[7], the future of work, and state revenues have led to the realisation that African countries are not as poor as is sometimes presumed.

---

[1] Owino (2019)
[2] See African Union Department of Economic Affairs, Waris and Magara (2019) trade dataset that is analysed and accessible in the companion website to this book housed at the Committee on Fiscal Studies, University of Nairobi Law School, at www.cfs.uonbi.ac.ke.
[3] United Nations (2000)
[4] United Nations (2015a)
[5] See www.addistaxinitiative.net
[6] See generally African Union and UNECA (2015) and Waris (2017c)
[7] Mwencha (2019) and Elmi (2019)

The world has recently been through several national, regional, continental and global economic depressions, especially those of 2009 and 2016.[8] These global economic crises coupled with poor and often biased management of domestic fiscal systems have undermined the ability of states and the African continent to be fiscally self-sufficient.

The proverb at the outset of this Introduction to *Financing Africa* suggests what may happen if we are not careful in handling fiscal and other resources on the continent. Let us not wait for the well to be empty.

For government revenue to be redistributed, it must first be taken away. To "give" and "take away" requires a whole set of fiscal laws, regulations, and policies at subnational, state, regional and continental levels and even within a governance institution or body. However, in African societies, we are barely familiar with taxation processes. This book moves forward on the premise that we must show how government spending takes place, to make the case for what a government wants to take away. This very delicate balance is the seesaw between the ability of people to pay and the right to receive services in support of decent living standards and development.

Resources that are taken and then given are governed by fiscal law and policy. Fiscal laws at the domestic level concern government expenditures, revenues, debt and taxation. All countries in the world including developing countries annually have increases in some sources of revenue and decreases in others.[9] State policy, determined politically with each incoming regime, not only prioritises from where certain revenue is collected but also plays the greatest role in determining how it is spent, i.e. on what expenditure priorities. Fiscal law situates itself during the fluctuating and at times unstable collection and redistribution of state revenue, which is a constant

---

[8] It is important to note that normally when an economic crisis happens in the global north, the real ripple effects hit Africa often three to five years later; the 2009 crisis really hit African states in 2012-2015. Arguably Africa may not yet have felt the full brunt of the 2016 fiscal crisis.
[9] Bird and Zolt (2003)

challenge for all those involved in the process, including nations, institutions, and organizations.

Anywhere in the world, violence, conflict, inadequate resources, poor management, and corruption can lead to a failure by states to collect revenue and use it properly. This results in the weak fiscal legitimacy of a state. If broken, a fiscal system, at local or global levels, can experience weaknesses in transparency, accountability, responsibility, efficiency, effectiveness, fairness and justice.[10] These principles are important if we are to ensure that the well does not run dry.

The balance between revenue and resource collection on the one hand and revenue and resource redistribution on the other is maintained and rests on the fiscal provisions in a nation's or an institution's constitution, legislation, regulations and policy, as well as any international commitments it makes including, but not limited to, treaties and contracts with the private sector.

A constitution should reflect the fiscal capacity of the state.[11] Supporting legislation must be in place, to elaborate on the application of the constitution, and may be subject to amendment to reflect needed changes. Regulation is attached to provisions of the law to better elaborate upon them for purposes of administration within a civil service. Policy is codified and implemented and amended from time to time based on need and the political thinking of the ruling government, usually in line with the party manifesto or platform. Treaties and other international commitments and contracts need to be reflected in the constitution, legislation, regulation and policies of the state. Best practices, standards and recommendations emerge from practitioners to elaborate upon, ease and clarify processes and elucidate emerging issues.

What exactly should be in a constitution? Should there be specific mentions of taxing rights or powers? Should there be debt ceilings? Should the budget proportions be pre-set? No single African country to date has a debt limit or ceiling constitutionally set out. Aid is not

---

[10] Waris (2013a)
[11] Waris (2015)

discussed at all in public fora and government business is similarly unelaborated and often opaque.

Taxation has a more varied treatment.[12] In Namibia, the government structure is established in two provisions in the constitution, with no mention of the word 'tax' nor 'taxation' although there is legislation related to taxation.[13] In the Senegalese constitution, there is a reference to tax but no clear sign of a taxpayers' duty or a governments' right to tax. The Senegalese constitution also states, in its second title, that any discrimination between men and women in employment, salary and taxation is forbidden.[14] There is also a reference to tax when setting out the relations between the executive power and the legislative power. It elaborates on rules and modalities of collecting taxes of all natures and provides currency guidelines.[15]

Legislation ideally should be anchored in a constitutional provision, but we can already see this is not necessarily the case in African countries.[16] However, the legislation can have policy and regulatory elaborations. There is, however, no real rhythm to this in African countries. Policies and regulations seem sometimes to be based on thinking in real time under a variety of influences.

Senegal's 2014-2035 development strategy is based on three pillars: (1) structural transformation of the economy by the consolidation of current engines of growth, creation of new sectors, boosting of exports and attraction of investment; (2) improving the wellbeing of the population, acting against the social inequality and supporting the emergence of viable regions and (3) reinforcement of security, stability, rights and liberties and the consolidation of the rule of law to create better conditions for social peace.[17] While laudable,

---

[12] Waris (2015)

[13] Republic of Namibia (2018)

[14] Republic of Senegal (2001) article 25. See also Waris (2019)

[15] Republic of Senegal (2001) article 67 and Republic of Guinea (2010) at article 22 of the constitution: *"Chaque citoyen doit contribuer, dans la mesure de ses moyens, à l'impôt et doit remplir ses obligations sociales pour le bien commun dans les conditions que la loi détermine"* (Each citizen must contribute taxes based on their ability in order to meet social obligations in accordance with the law).

[16] Waris (2015)

[17] Republic of Senegal (2010) p. 6

this strategy has not been supported with rules and regulations, making it difficult to see whether the fiscal allocations within budgets are reflecting the ambitions set out.

This brief canvas of constitution, law, regulation and policy and how they interrelate reveals already a problem in the conceptualization and coherence of fiscal law and policy. States do not follow the basis of the law. There is little coherence. Laws and policies seem to be an accident of fate or history and do not fit into the jigsaw puzzle of what should be the regulatory framework of a state. The laws and policies, which are disconnected from the constitutions, seem to reflect pressures from colonial legacies, donors and consultants and often a lack a guiding philosophy.[18]

A common presumption is that revenue and expenditure is a tedious, mysterious world of codes and numbers, and is a matter for experts of which there are allegedly none on the African continent. The intention behind this book is to first, make apparent how fiscal law, regulation and policy should, could or ought to operate; second, illustrate the diverse approaches African states' have taken in their fiscal systems; and third, make some recommendations on how a state can have a good fiscal system, ensure that all revenues due to the state are collected and expenditures prioritized, build a good fiscal architecture at subnational, national, regional, continental and global levels, and be cognisant of global, continental and regional commitments.

The book will not explore in depth the regional, continental and global system in place but refer to it periodically where relevant, from a domestic perspective. Using publicly available data, it provides a snapshot of the diversity in fiscal approaches being pursued as pushes towards harmonisation and integration intensify.

This introductory chapter will describe the global challenges facing fiscal systems. It then maps out the status of the fiscal system in Africa, based on available data, and outlines the challenges facing African states. In unpacking the status of the domestic fiscal system on the continent, it is hoped that the reader will be positioned to

---

[18] Waris (2019)

assess whether the well is empty or not, and if not how low the water level is in the well.

1.1. Unpacking government resources and the balance with expenditure[19]

When the data on illicit financial flows (IFF) and tax non-compliance began emerging in the media in the early 2000s, the line between states that were perceived to be weakly governed[20] and those with strong governance seemed to be clearly drawn. The difference between a corrupt and a less corrupt nation similarly seemed clear.[21] Since the early 2000s, with the release of the Financial Secrecy Index (FSI)[22] and numerous leaks and scandals such as LuxLeaks[23], WikiLeaks[24], SwissLeaks[25], Panama papers[26] and most recently the Paradise papers[27] and the Mauritius Leaks[28], it has become glowingly clear that concerns around weak governance are global and that no country has remained untouched by problems of fiscal compliance and corruption.

These problems impede the ability of states to finance the sustainable development goals (SDGs), poverty alleviation, development and to achieve and maintain fiscal self-sufficiency. This inability of states to self-finance is further exacerbated by unregulated technology-related spaces and the ability of individuals and companies engaging with technology to expedite financial transactions and obfuscate them, increasing the size of the shadow economy.[29] These global scandals and technological developments

---

[19] Parts of this section were previously published in German in Waris (2018b)
[20] Mo Ibrahim Foundation (2017)
[21] Transparency International (2017)
[22] Tax Justice Network (2018)
[23] ICIJ (2014)
[24] WikiLeaks (2015)
[25] ICIJ (2016)
[26] ICIJ (2018)
[27] ICIJ (2017)
[28] ICIJ (2019)
[29] UNCTAD (2019)

are emerging in a world where some countries have high and stable fiscal revenue and others have very little fiscal stability.[30]

In addition to taxes, states traditionally rely on state revenue from government business, loans, aid and rent from natural resources. The principles in this book that will be discussed could be applied to any state resource or expenditure, not just to taxation and its redistribution. A difference among these forms of revenue is that, while the amount of resources obtained from loans, aid and government business can be determined through a negotiated contract, often in law or between the negotiating parties, the same is not applicable to tax and state expenditure.

The absence of a regularly renegotiated fiscal social contract between a country's population and its government is a policy gap, creates space for maladministration, and leads to loopholes for both the taxpayer and the tax collector as well as those in government redistributing or spending.

A continual challenge for any government in the world is that few states have a constitutional or legally prescribed maximum limit regarding the amount of tax that can be collected or even a debt limit. The fiscal social contract is the closest one gets to this. The concept is not necessarily alive in the minds of people unless lived through a constitution-making process which included them. For example, the process in Eritrea from 1997 to date remains incomplete.[31] Even when the process is complete, the elaboration and implementation of legislation is usually left to the executive, and the parliament is expected to codify this in regulation and policy. In the case of Eritrea, the failure of the President to assent to the constitution means there has been no implementation of the voice of the people.

Defining the limit to fiscal revenue and how it is spent is a real challenge. The only measure of a high, and often by extension oppressive fiscal system, is public discontent, outcry and the threat of, or actual, revolt by the people.[32] While there are ways to measure

---

[30] The internet today is predominantly controlled by four companies (Google, Amazon, Facebook and Apple), all headquartered in the USA with the result that the large proportion of fiscal revenue is collected there.

[31] Mekonnen (2015)

[32] Burg (2004)

the willingness of a people to be taxed and contribute, the people and society base willingness on how state resources are spent. The resting point is that revenue should be kept at a basic minimum, and most tend to say: no tax is a good tax. Despite this, there are reasons for resources to be collected, but what remains crucial is the holistic fiscal system in which the revenue and expenditure of the state is designed and balanced. A state could have high revenue collections but only if the spending is on the people and to their overall satisfaction.

Sabine[33] argues that we can have taxation without government, but we cannot have government without taxation. This argument has been recently evidenced by the fact that Belgium, for many years, ran a state with taxation but no government. One could extend this argument to say that a government could also run even without the day to day presence of the president. In Cameroon, it is a well-known fact that President Biya often resides in Geneva, Switzerland. South Sudan and Somalia, while in conflict situations, had had their entire parliament if not their cabinet living in Nairobi. Resources, including tax, finance the socioeconomic and political development of a society. Taxation is a central function of government.

Paying tax hurts taxpayers when it is perceived as the compulsory removal of money that taxpayers feel they have worked hard to earn and is being collected excessively from both formal and informal sources (like both government and local mafias) or is being misspent. Taxes it is argued should never leave more than that most basic and inevitable sense of injustice that we feel when we are compelled to give money to the government whether we like it or not. Additionally, states and their arms of enforcement ought to be reasonable, just and fair in reaching their decision to tax. The individual wishes the government to achieve, on his or her behalf, the least taxation for the maximum effect on those packages of expenditure in public life that have been deemed to be more effectively and more economically carried out by the public purse, similar to the balancing of a household budget.

Fairness and justice in tax collection and expenditure is part of the validation of a fiscal system and its ability to continue operating.

---

[33] Sabine (1991)

To achieve this fairness and justice, people must have a clear participatory role in determining the level of revenue collection and its redistribution. People witness redistribution of the entire state budget and the spending of all resources whether from tax, loans, aid or government business. A government that is a true representative of the taxpayer values the trust and understanding of the people and their consent to use the money collected wisely on behalf of the whole community according to principles of distributive justice and the common good.[34]

Unjust taxes are ultimately uncollectible. At best, one cannot expect even just taxes to gain more than a grudging acceptance from the public. Not everyone will always be satisfied with tax, because at best it is always a suboptimal compromise between competing interests and the resource requirements of the state. Demonstrations have taken place in South Africa against the implementation of a road toll and in Kenya against the implementation of fuel levies and the price of electricity. The public is essential if a state is to sustain a society in which there is: peace, security, an unbiased justice system, a good education system, universal healthcare, low-income housing, food security, universal adult suffrage, consistent and forward-looking poverty reduction strategies, growth of wealth, rising living standards, and development.

The duty of government is not only to raise taxes that are necessary to avoid all social ills, which are self-evidently unacceptable and divisive, but also to use strategies around fiscal resources to ensure all members of society grow and prosper. No matter which way one looks, states require resources.[35]

According to a proverb from Nigeria, "a horse has four legs, yet it often falls." Similarly, while we are clear that states require resources and have the right to receive them, the planning of how to achieve growth and prosperity of an entire society remains a challenge. This is perhaps the weakest leg of the horse.

Many scholars argue that we must first look at collection before we make spending decisions, and others believe it is vice versa.

---

[34] Waris (2013a) chapters 1 and 2; Alt (2019)
[35] Waris (2018b)

Deciding on which leg to stand at a given point in time can be a matter of opinion. This book will move forward on the premise that we should first question the way in which we collect and spend existing revenue before we make attempts to increase revenue through new forms, whether from government business, loans, aid, revenue collection or even increased rates of tax. Economical and effective use of already available funds is what leads to compliant taxpayers and a peaceful society.

Some ask if government revenue and taxation can be more effectively carried out if it is not undertaken by the government but by an individual or in smaller groups, however data shows that the only thing that actually changes is the beneficiaries.[36] You need financial inclusion in order to finance development in a stable way, but to do so one needs to understand the context of the state for which the fiscal system is being designed and ensure its procurement and tender system is a true reflection.[37]

1.2. Understanding the 54 countries that make up the African continent

While moving towards a simpler, more equitable, transparent and broad-based fiscal system has been a concern for developing countries for decades, even the most basic understanding of a system can sometimes be overwhelming. Not only are there global benchmarks, there are also African continental positions to which states have acquiesced but which they have not implemented.

In addition, documents like the African Charter as well as diverse subsequent declarations have mapped out the basic requirements that each individual African country ought to achieve. Treaties that form the basis of the fiscal system at the continental level include the Constitutive Act of the African Union; African Charter of Human and People's Rights (ACHPR) (1981); Abuja Declaration on Health Spending (ADHS) (2001); African Convention on Preventing and Combatting Corruption (ACPCC) (2003); Maputo Declaration on

---

[36] Akech (2006)
[37] Thiankolu (2019)

Agriculture and Food Security (MDAFS) (2003); African Charter on Democracy Elections and Governance (2007); African Charter on Statistics (ACS) (2009); African Charter on the Values and Principles of Public Service and Administration (ACVPPSA) (2011); and African Charter on the Values and Principles of Decentralisation, Local Governance and Local Development (ACVPDLGLD) (2014).

These treaties together give guidance on the quality of information being collected, how populations are to be treated, and controls on what government can do – controls on government responsibility as well as that of public servants. The treaties support the movement of states towards decentralisation, requiring states to transfer power, responsibilities, capacities and resources to the subnational level.

Table 1. Expected African state budget framework based on continental commitments

Revenue	%	Expenditure	%
Taxation	?	Health	15% of budget
Debt/Loans	?	Agriculture and food security	10% of budget
Aid	?	Education	?
Non-tax revenue	?	Social welfare	?
Government business	?	Infrastructure	?
Royalties	?	Security	?
		Research	1% of GDP
		Membership dues: African Union	0.2% of customs
		Debt financing	?
		Devolved expenditure	?
		Central government expenditure	?
Total	100%		100%

Source: Author

They stipulate that each country must spend a minimum of 15% of its national budget on health and 10% on agriculture and food security and that an import levy of 0.2% will be imposed on eligible imports for the financing of the African Union. Via these treaties and laws, a compliant African government has limited its own powers by stating prioritized expenditures. In Table 1 is the framework for a national budget on the African continent if an African state complies with the African obligations set out above.

The continent can only be understood in its diversity. This section sets out to reflect the diverse positions of individual African states, despite continental and global commitments. It looks at participation in budgeting processes, economic growth, taxation, debt and, state expenditure. There was difficulty in identifying aid and government business definitively as well as expenditure policy.

1.2.1. Participation, budgeting and access to information

Participation is not equally open to all members of a state or society. Almost every country in the world today has fiscal laws, regulations, and policies and that are a vast playground for special interests.[38] Well funded, well networked, and/or knowledgeable lobby groups argue for exemptions and use loopholes to reduce the tax burdens of those represent, leading to special treatment and issues of evasion, avoidance and tax planning.[39] This skewing of the purposes of public participation has opened up debates on the ethics and morality of taxation.

In Tanzania, in line with the ACVPDLGLD, article 146 of the constitution says:

> The purpose of having local government authorities is to transfer authority to the people. Local government authorities shall have the right [...] to involve the people, in the planning and implementation of development programmes [...][40]

Other countries with participatory requirements in their constitutions in 2016 included: Kenya, South African, Tanzania Tunisia, and Zimbabwe.[41] Guinea has a presidential system which is strongly centralised. However, the budget is an annual participatory process involving administration at all levels, development partners,

---

[38] Waris (2017b)
[39] Tutt (1985)
[40] Crawford and Hartmann (2008) p. 164
[41] Fuo (2015) p. 169

Parliament, private sector and organizations of the civil society at different levels.[42] Citizens are entitled to:

- Assistance concerning the budget or following them at national and local levels;
- Participation at all events to meet the responsible during community work;
- Visit offices of administration services and meet the leaders to collect information on the public resources that affect them and discuss their concerns; and
- Access to a paper or online version of the budget guide or the budget of the state.

Figure 1. Map of African countries with participatory budget processes in 2016

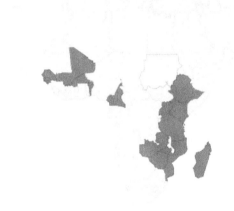

1 ▓▓▓▓▓▓▓▓▓▓▓▓▓▓ 1

Source: Author

The countries highlighted in Figure 1 are those that have legislated participation in budgetary processes. As at 2016, public participation was only possible in 15 out of the 54 African countries: Senegal, Gambia, Guinea Bissau, Mali, Burkina Faso, Benin, Cameroon, Ethiopia, Kenya, Uganda, Tanzania, Mozambique, Zambia, Zimbabwe and Madagascar.

The right to access information generally as well as accessing budgetary information allows citizens to fully participate in the

---

[42] Republic of Guinea (2017) p. 21

budget process. The new policy of the Guinean minister of budget is to make that right exercisable, with a view to strengthen budgetary transparency and materialize the political will of the President of the Republic to put the national budget at the service of the citizens. The Guinean budget guide was published for the first time in 2017.

Despite this apparently positive picture of access to information and participation, states are not implementing the law especially in the context of fiscal information. For example, in Kenya, despite constitutionally mandated participation, a treaty was concluded and then challenged in court; the civil society organization that took the matter to court won, however another treaty has already been concluded, again without societal participation.[43]

Figure 2. Map of African countries with freedom of information laws in 2016

1 ▬▬▬▬▬▬▬ 1

Source: Author

Highlighted in Figure 2 are the 11 African countries that by 2016, had passed national freedom of information laws: Guinea, Sierra Leone, Liberia, Nigeria, Niger, Ethiopia, Uganda, Rwanda, Angola, Zimbabwe, and South Africa. These are not all the same countries that allow for participatory budgeting. Some countries like Angola

---

[43] Picciotto (2019)

14

have freedom of information laws in place but not participatory budgeting, and in Madagascar there are provisions for participation but no freedom of information.

Even where there is freedom of information, this may not necessarily include access to financial data, state to business contracts, tenders or the procurement process. This raises the question: How can there be effective public participation if access to information rights are not in place or vice versa? Checks and balances beyond participatory budgeting become an even greater challenge.

1.2.2. African economic growth

The commencement point of a developed country may be different from that of a developing country. Nigeria and South Africa account for nearly 50% of the continent's GDP (at 29.3% and 19.1% respectively). However, on a regional level the share of growth skews in favour of eastern Africa as illustrated in Figures 3 and 4.

Figure 3. GDP growth by region on the African continent in 2016

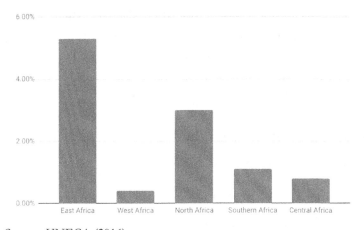

Source: UNECA (2016)

Figure 4: Share of African GDP growth by region in 2016

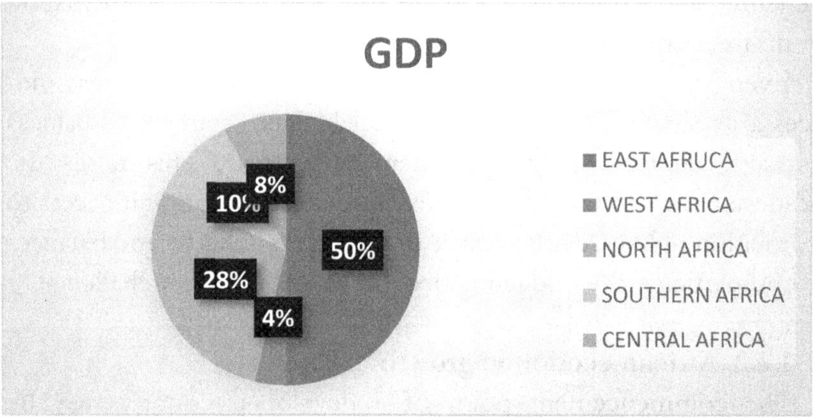

Source: UNECA 2016

It is estimated that East Africa's economy expanded by 5.3% in 2016, accounting for 50% of the continent's economic growth. Although this is slower than the previous year's rate of 6.5%, it is still by far the fastest growing region in Africa. Ethiopia, which grew by 8%, was the leading country in the region; Kenya, Rwanda, Tanzania and Djibouti all managed growth rates above 6% in 2016.

North Africa was the second fastest growing region (at 3%), followed by southern Africa (1.1%), and then Central Africa (0.8%). GDP growth in West Africa reached only 0.4%, a result of a recession in Nigeria where GDP contracted by 1.5% (from 2.8% in 2015).

Botswana and eSwatini (Swaziland) are the only two countries in Africa which did not record deficits in their 2016 account balances. The rest are net importers of goods and services. Estimates show that 20 of the 54 countries had double-digit current account deficits in 2016, with the highest in Libya (37.8% of GDP) and Mozambique (31.1% of GDP).

Growth, for state financing purposes, usually translates into how much more revenue the state ought to be able to collect as a result of the economy growing. If West African growth reached 0.4% during a recession it means that without any increased taxes at all, the governments in West Africa should almost naturally collect at least 0.3% more revenue in the following year.

In 2018, 92% of announced foreign firect investment (FDI) in greenfield (new) projects went to 10 African countries. These countries were Egypt, Morocco, Angola, Ghana, Mozambique, Ethiopia, South Africa, Nigeria, Tanzania and Kenya. Morocco leads cross-border capital investment in the African continent, with about $8bn announced for 2015-2016. Ethiopia received over $3bn for a fertiliser factory. The second largest recipient of Morocco's FDI is Cote d'Ivoire ($2.7bn in 2015-2016).

Africa's FDI flows to the rest of the world declined in 2016, reversing a trend seen over the last few years, and this despite the push by Kenya in 2012 to create an international financial centre.[44] The continent's largest investor abroad, South Africa, saw its outflows drop by 30% and 58% in 2015 and 2016 respectively. Nigeria's investment outside the continent has also been in decline since 2015.[45] Ideally this means that illicit financial outflows should similarly be reducing or be flowing more to other states within the African continent.

Table 2. Major investments in Africa, in 2016

Country investing	Countries of investment	Industries	Amount in 2016
Morocco	Ethiopia Cote d'Ivoire	Fertilizer	8 billion USD 2.7 billion USD
China		Land	38.4 billion USD
United Arab Emirates (UAE)		Al Habtoor	14.9 billion USD
Italy		Oil and gas	11.6 billion USD

Source: Author

Fortune Land Development was the largest investor in Africa in the 2015-2016 period, followed by the UAE-based conglomerate, Al Habtoor Group, and Eni SpA, an Italian oil and gas multinational corporation (MNC). Overall, Chinese firms contributed $38.4bn to African greenfield projects for the period. UAE-based firms invested $14.9bn, and Italian firms committed $11.6bn in total. See Table 2.

---

[44] Waris (2014b)
[45] African Union Department of Economic Affairs, Waris and Magara (2019)

Companies from the USA came in fourth place, investing around $10.4bn.

Knowing what country is investing in what helps countries strategize about trade relationships. Countries neighbouring the countries of investment should question why they are not receiving similar funding.

Data on investments were difficult to locate and often out of date. This may reflect the fact that private investor related data may not be collected in a regular and organised manner, and if incentives or exemptions were given may also not be monitored as a result.

The African continent has the highest proportion of adults who are starting or running new businesses. The decline in extractive resources as sources of growth is reflected across most of Africa. In 2015, the five fastest-growing economies were non-resource rich, with Ethiopia, Cote d'Ivoire and Rwanda at 10.2%, 8.8% and 7.1%, respectively. Oil now accounts for 10% of Nigeria's GDP, down from 25.6% in 2000 (although it still contributes to over 90% of foreign exchange earnings). In Nigeria, oil revenues are also now down to 50% of total state revenue, and 50% was sourced from taxation as of 2018, however the veracity of this information remains unclear because data on aid and loans is difficult to ascertain.

1.2.3. Taxation in Africa

Between January and December 2018, data collected by the author directly from government sources as well as revenue authorities and continental fiscal institutions showed a huge disparity even in the identification of taxpayers. The challenges in accessing this data and the peculiar lack of detail shows several challenges immediately facing African countries, their governments and their people in trying to ensure better governance and push towards improved fiscal legitimacy.

Country data on the numbers of people over the age of 18 was not accessible; as a result, voter data was collected. Elections in different countries on the continent happen at different times, and therefore the data is not a very reliable comparison, however this is the only information publicly available. For the 20 countries for which the data was accessible, a comparison was made with the number of registered taxpayers, individuals and corporations combined. This is because most countries, apart from Kenya, did not have data on how many corporate income and personal income taxpayers had filed returns in 2018 or even how many individual taxpayers were registered as opposed to companies and other taxable entities.[46] The percentages are illustrated in Table 3 and Figure 5.

Table 3. Taxpayers registered as a percentage of registered voters, in selected African countries as of December 2018

Country	% of voters registered for tax	Country	% of voters registered for tax
Angola	39%	Namibia	55%
Cameroon	7%	Nigeria	4%
Egypt	14%	Senegal	1%
Gambia	17%	Seychelles	35%
Ghana	10%	South Africa	99%
Kenya	39%	Swaziland (Eswatini)	8%
Liberia	2%	Tanzania	11%
Madagascar	3%	Togo	2%
Malawi	0.2%	Uganda	7%
Mauritius	63%	Zambia	4%

Source: Author

Figure 5. Taxpayers registered as a percentage of registered voters, in selected African countries as of December 2018

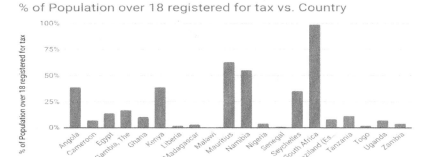

Source: Author

---

[46] ATAF, Waris and Magara (2019)

The data, despite its weaknesses, shows cause for concern. The average age of an African today is 19 years, and most African countries do not have social welfare such as unemployment benefits or even pensions that can be called a living wage, with the result that the financial burden on the working population is likely very large. The data also points to the well known fact that there is a huge informal sector made up of unregistered businesses that are run like registered businesses. Although in other continents there may be micro and small size businesses, in African countries these tend to be small and medium size businesses being run unregistered in order to avoid government regulations.

The registered taxpayer (individuals and corporations) population seems to vary from 0.2% of the population in Malawi and 1% in Senegal, to 11% in Tanzania and 14% in Egypt, and to 35% in the Seychelles, 55% in Namibia, and 99% in South Africa. Clearly this disparity shows that the tax base is severely limited in most African countries, and that only a select part of the population is paying corporate and personal income tax. Only a few countries had available corporation data, but it made little or no change to the analysis presented in Table 3 and Figure 5. However, all people making formal purchases are paying indirect taxes like value-added tax (VAT).

This data begs the question of why more people and corporations are not being added to the income tax base. It seems that there is high unemployment, however there is a higher probability that many of the unregistered taxpayers are in the informal sector and others are students or pensioners, but still, this does not account for the wide disparities in the numbers.

Figure 6. Mapping of taxpayer registration as a percent of registered voters, as of December 2018

0.002 ▆▆▆▆▆▆▆▆▆ 0.99

Source: Author

As mapped in Figure 6, we see that taxpayer registration is very low (10% or less of registered voters) in West and Central Africa, as well as in some countries in East and southern Africa. Access to data is crucial in understanding taxpayers and the size of the fiscal purse.

Access to information on domestic and foreign corporations is also important, however, many African countries were unable to provide or have never publicly released data on the number of state-owned corporations, and even fewer have data on domestic and foreign corporations.

Table 4. Number of foreign corporations in (9) African countries, as of December 2018

Country	Number of foreign corporations	Country	Number of foreign corporations
Burundi	31	Malawi	34
Chad	8	Mozambique	9
Gambia	6,471	Rwanda	150
Ghana	568	Swaziland (Eswatini)	23
Liberia	79		

Source: Author

Figure 7. Graph of number of foreign corporations in (9) African countries, as of December 2018

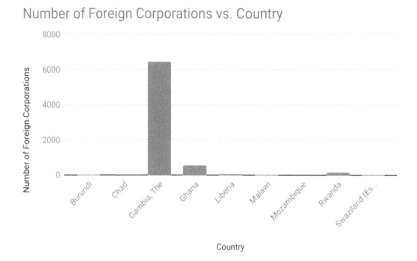

Source: Author

Figure 8: Mapping of number of foreign corporations in (9) African countries, as of December 2018

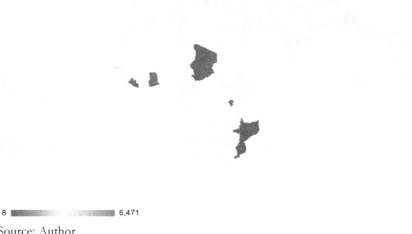

8 ▬▬▬▬▬▬▬▬▬ 6,471

Source: Author

Table 4 and Figures 7 and 8 show that out of the nine African countries for which data was available, the number of foreign corporations in countries ranges from 8 in Chad to almost 6,500 in Gambia. This does not, however, reflect the corporations' contributions to the state resource pool. Unlike developed countries, some of the poorest countries rely very heavily on corporate tax revenue from MNCs. It is therefore critical that developing countries can tax the full revenues (of individuals and corporations) that are realized in their jurisdictions. However, if data is not available on the number of corporations and their revenues, how can we adequately draw up the fiscal design of the system most suited for that state?

Further analysis showed that indirect taxes have a great influence on collections. For example, in Namibia the tax revenue is significant, accounts for over 90% of the budget. But, if the income of the Southern African Customs Union (SACU) is excluded, the proportion is about 65% of the budget.[47] Namibia legislated a minimum salary in 2014 of $888 per month (+/- $26 a day). The country also has an exemption of taxation for all yearly income under 50,000 Namibian dollars.[48]

---

[47] Republic of Namibia (2017)
[48] Republic of Namibia (2016)

In 2007, Namibia already had a subsidy programme for production inputs and services for communal farmers in dryland crop production. In addition, Namibia has state-owned enterprises (SOEs) such as banks, airports and water companies in addition to a social security and telecommunication commission.[49] Data on SOEs including the amount of revenue they generate for the state and that is put into the budget remains unclear.

Data collected, often with difficulty, and shared in Appendix C, shows that all African countries own at least one business enterprise in its entirety and tend to be shareholders in several other companies. The industries they invest in include telecommunications, extractives, and services as well as agriculture and even construction. Data on mining in the extractives sector, aid, loans, and stolen asset recovery similarly difficult to collect and showed a lack of transparency. Data was scanty in newspaper articles and showed no reflection of improved budgeting or reductions in revenue authority targets. The table in Appendix D shows data, that was publicly available, on to African countries. What could not be ascertained was the exact amount of total profit states are receiving from business investment as well as the total amount of aid they received.

1.2.4. African debt

Data for 2018 shows that several African countries, including the Republic of Congo, Mozambique, Eritrea, Somalia, South Sudan, Sudan and Zimbabwe, are in debt distress. Zambia and the Central African Republic were at high risk in the 2000s when Africa's debt was mostly composed of multilateral and bilateral concessional loans.

In 2005, Tanzania's debt was increasing whilst tax revenue collection remained low at 10.8% of GDP. To address this, the government with the support of the World Bank embarked on a project to make the Tanzania Revenue Authority more efficient and effective in its administration of taxes.[50] The project, known as the Tax Modernization Project, improved the country's tax infrastructure. Revenue collection improved at an average annual rate

---

[49] Sornarajah (2010) p. 40
[50] World Bank (2012)

of 21% from 2007 to 2011. E-filing of VAT returns increased from less than 500 in 2009 to over 4,000 in 2011. A total of 376,666 taxpayers registered with a newly introduced mobile tax payment for property taxes.

Chad witnessed a contraction in oil revenue as well as a heavy debt service burden for external commercial debt, resulting in spending cuts and the suspension of tax exemptions. Non-oil resources in Chad stand at 5% of the GDP. To respond to budgetary and debt obligations, Chad engaged in a reform of non-oil tax revenue resources as follows:

- Strengthening core tax administration functions such as tax registration and identification of new taxpayers; as part of this reform an automated tax administration system was rolled out in 2014;
- Modernization and simplification of the tax filing payment procedures; and
- Increased and improved collection of excise revenues.

Several African countries (including Chad, Sudan, Mozambique, Benin, Kenya and Zimbabwe) are facing debt-to-GDP ratios above the 50% mark. In Benin, internal and external debt as a share of GDP amounted to 47.6% in 2016 and 54.6% in 2017, an increase of 7% in the period of one year. Several countries have also begun to issue international bonds to raise revenue. The share of bonds in total external public and publicly guaranteed debt increased from 9% in 2007 to 19% in 2016 in African countries (excluding North Africa).

The increasing level of debt poses a significant risk for sustainable development. It places pressure on national revenue authorities to collect more tax to finance the debt and has caused governments to reduce financing for sustainable development initiatives. Furthermore, the failure to collect enough revenue through tax results in budget deficits that have forced governments to resort to potentially regressive measures to raise revenue needed to meet debt obligations. In Kenya, for instance, increased debt resulted in the government initiating aggressive tax changes in 2018, aimed at raising revenue to meet the upcoming debt obligations. The changes include introduction of VAT on petroleum at a rate of 18%.

The Government of Ghana increased its commitment to mobilize domestic public resources by, among other actions, addressing excessive tax incentives particularly in extractive industries. It is estimated that tax incentives cost the economy about 4% to 5% of GDP between 2016 and 2017.[51] This implies that Ghana is losing a significant portion of potential tax revenue to the tax exemption and incentive regime. An 8% increase in excise on telecommunication services, mobile money transactions, and financial services offered by banks has been introduced. Despite strengthened debt management procedures in most countries, this has so far not spurred growth, improved living standards, or alleviated poverty in countries such as Mozambique, Angola or Zambia where debt levels remain relatively high.

With a continued rise in global interest rates, external financing conditions are expected to become more challenging for African countries, and capital flows are expected to decline. Interest rate increases raise debt service costs, which are already high for many countries. African countries need to enhance resilience through an appropriate mix of fiscal, monetary, exchange rate and prudential policies to reduce vulnerability to the tightening global financial conditions, currency fluctuations and capital outflows. Close monitoring of the effects of global trends on areas such as the public and private sector balance sheets and domestic inflation is critical.

Such monitoring should include analysis of fiscal and debt sustainability and the impact of debt management on growth and investment. The Angolan government introduced macroeconomic stabilization programmes aimed at improving the business environment through deficit reduction and debt consolidation and greater exchange rate flexibility. Angola and South Africa, the two largest economies of southern Africa, are expected to grow at 2% and 1.4%, respectively, in 2018. In 2018, growth performance in the region continued to be driven by economies such as Botswana, Malawi, Mauritius and Zambia, growing at 4.4%, 4.4%, 3.7% and 4.1%, respectively.

---

[51] Mensah (2015)

African countries' commitment to meeting Vision 2063 of the African Union as well as the SDGs seems to have strengthened their resolve to closing the infrastructure deficit on the continent, leading to increased borrowing, particularly in North and East Africa. This has led to an increase in overall continental total external debt share in GDP, rising from an estimated 35.5% in 2017 to 37.6% in 2018. This contributes significantly to the continent's high public debt levels (at 51% of GDP in 2018), especially in oil importing countries where it hoovers above 60% of GDP in some cases. Total external debt among oil exporters more than doubled as a share of GDP, rising from a low of 13.1% in 2015 to 28.3% in 2018. This exacerbates the continental picture, even as total external debt in oil importing countries has remained broadly stable, albeit at high levels of just under 45% of GDP.

1.2.5. State expenditure

Data shows that over half of African countries still mobilize less than 15% of their GDP in tax revenues, below the minimum level of 20% considered by the UN as necessary to achieve the MDGs by 2015.[52] Since 2015, the new targets of the SDGs have specific fiscally related provisions but no clear provisions at domestic, regional, or continental levels. This is left to individual states and regional blocs.

Africa's resource envelope of public social expenditure compares relatively well globally. On average, about 30% of total public expenditure is allocated to social services, compared to 21% in developed countries.[53] However, there is a substantial variation across African countries. In Nigeria, for example, close to 20% of consolidated average government expenditure went towards health, education, skills training and social protection over the 10-year period of 2006-2016. In Kenya, social spending decreased from 39.7% of government expenditure in 2012-2013 to 25.18% in 2016-2017.

Several health expenditure targets have been agreed upon globally. In 2001, a minimum of $34 per capita expenditure on health was recommended by the WHO Commission on Macroeconomic

---

[52] Waris and Kohonen (2011)
[53] OECD (2016b)

Health, and in 2009, the High Level Taskforce (HLTF) for Innovative International Financing for Health Systems recommended $44 per capita as the minimum health expenditure needed to introduce essential interventions to reach increased coverage rates by 2017. With the SDGs, another costing was done that estimated the need at $217 per capita on average, as envisaged in the Addis Ababa Action Agenda. African countries have made progress towards the global goal of $44 per capita in expenditures for health. Expenditures on health have increased over time, with a reduction in the number of African countries spending less than $20 per capita.

The African Union heads of state, in 2001 in Abuja, set a health spending target of 15% of total government expenditure. The performance of African countries against this spending threshold is less remarkable than the per capita spending. There seems to be a lack of prioritization of health spending within national budgets, as government expenditure on health as a share of total expenditure remained at round 10% during 2006-2014.

Even with increased per capita spending, the burden of healthcare has been borne by out-of-pocket spending. The performance of African countries against both the Abuja target and the global $44 per capita target is quite revealing. Only five countries (Botswana, Rwanda, Zambia, Madagascar and Togo) (see Figures 9 and 10) have so far met the Abuja target, and of these, only the first three have met the HLTF target of $44 per capita. The increase in health expenditure per capita, which includes both private and public health spending, reveals large proportions of private spending to address poverty and inequality.

On average, African governments spend 2% of GDP on health, though with wide variation. Oil exporting countries allocate on average 1.5% of GDP to heath expenditures, and oil importing countries allocate on average 2.4% of GDP. Health expenditures have increased in some North African countries (i.e., Morocco, Tunisia and Algeria) and are as high as 5% of GDP in Namibia. But they are less than 1% of GDP in Nigeria, Equatorial Guinea, DRC and Cameroon.[54]

Figure 9. Percentage of GDP used on health spending

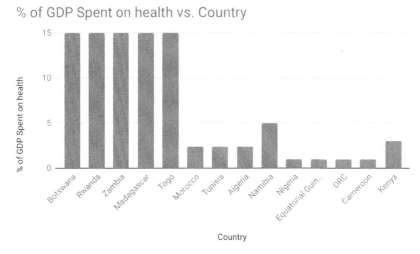

Source: Author

Figure 10. Mapping of percentage of GDP used on health pending

Source: Author

---

[54] Detailed research on how to make budgets more responsive to health can be found at www.Go4Health.eu

Social spending in Africa, whilst improving, retains a "cost-sharing" component with households, which in turn drives inequality of access to public goods and services and leads to catastrophic spending by households, particularly for health services. For example, out-of-pocket payments increased in nearly all African countries from $15 per capita in 1995 to $38 in 2014.[55] In Lesotho in 2001, between 1% and 3% of households faced catastrophic expenditures, because 40% of their monthly income was spent on health.[56]

The need for inclusive public expenditure on health is an important component in achieving the 2030 Agenda for Sustainable Development[57] and Agenda 2063: The Africa We Want[58]. Household expenditure on health was particularly high in 2000; in 23 of the 50 African countries with data, out-of-pocket spending represented an average of 45% of household spending, which dropped to 36% in 2015.[59] In 2015, African countries with higher GDP per capita had an out of pocket expenditure representing 70% of household spending, again demonstrating certain shortfalls in budget prioritization of health expenditure.

Patterns of spending on education are like those of spending on health. On average, African countries spend almost 2% of their GDP on education, with however disparities across oil importing and exporting groups. Oil importing countries spend a higher ratio of GDP on education: 3% on average between 2000 and 2015, as compared to their oil exporting counterparts (0.5% of GDP). Countries like Tunisia, Namibia, South Africa, Kenya, Burkina Faso, Niger and Cote d'Ivoire spend between 4% and 6% of GDP on education. Sudan, Central African Republic, Guinea Bissau and Zambia are among the countries that spend the least, about 1% of their GDP, on education. Nevertheless, average country spending in Africa has been close to the Fast Track Initiative recommended

---

[55] Beegle, Christiaensen, Dabalen and Gaddis (2016)
[56] Akinkugbe, Chana-Chiliba and Tlotlego (2012)
[57] United Nations (2015a) and United Nations (2015b)
[58] Africa Union (2013)
[59] UNECA (2018)

benchmark (of 20% of domestic spending directed towards education) set out in 2002 over the period of 1995 to 2016. The Fast Track Initiative was rebranded in 2011 as the Global Partnership for Education.

1.3. Core challenges to fiscal legitimacy in Africa[60]

> *When building a house,*
> *don't measure the timbers in the forest.*
>
> Proverb from Liberia

One cannot simply look at states' fiscal systems and point to issues. One must examine the systems and ensure they are the right choices for the task at hand. Similarly to the house and its timbers, the fiscal system must be considered in the historical, economic, socio-political, ideological, racial, ethnic, and belief systems in which it exists.[61] This section discusses ten challenges African states face when it comes to taxation, fiscal legitimacy, and the ability to collect and redistribute domestic resources.

First challenge. Most African countries comprise more than one ethnic community, and tribalism among them has prevented African states from uniting into one nation with one government for one people.[62] Nigeria has more than 250 ethnic groups.[63] South Africa has five racial population groups and 11 South African ethnic groups.[64] Kenya has 44 recognised ethnic communities[65], but according to national debates, there may be over 100 different ethnic communities.

Numerous allegations and grand corruption scandals in most African countries, evidenced recently in relation to the former Zuma administration in South Africa, reflect a form of state capture by certain ethnic communities, clans and families. Such tribalism retards

---

[60] Parts of this section were previously published in Waris (2018b)
[61] Mumford (2002) p. 219
[62] Khamisi (2018)
[63] United States Embassy in Nigeria (2012)
[64] Government of South Africa (2010)
[65] Republic of Kenya (2017)

the development of the state and the pooling and spending of resources for the common good. At independence in Tanzania, the Nyerere government refused to recognise the 100 ethnic communities and instead moved towards developing a collective Tanzanian consciousness. Tribalism further unpacks itself in governments in different African countries, where we have politicians voted in, often on ethnic cards. Implementing policies they do not believe in from a philosophical point of view is often difficult if not impossible.

Second challenge. Levels of exposure and compliance to the state have varied over time and within and among communities, leading to very different understandings of taxation. Within a country experiences differ, based on a variety of factors including distance from the capital city, urban and rural settings, settler and pastoral lifestyles, exposure to different ethnic communities, and association with oppositional forces as opposed to political leaders in power.

Historically, experiences have been varied, before, during and after colonisation – while keeping in mind that Ethiopia and Liberia were not colonised like other African countries. Some communities had a well-developed monetary and tax system financing the state. This was the case for example of Mombasa, Lamu and Malindi, which were among the city states along the East African coast[66] from present day Somalia to present day Madagascar. It was also the case of the city state of Benin along the Gulf of Guinea, and of the kingdoms of the Ashanti in current day Ghana and the Songhai in current day Mali.[67] We also find communities with forms of exchange of services, for example for security and conflict resolution. The warrior clan, for example the Kikuyu in Kenya, provided security and in return their families were housed and fed. In the case of the Banyarwanda, found in modern day Rwanda, Burundi, Uganda and DRC, they had a chief who administered and settled disputes in return for food.

Thus, peoples' fiscal knowledge varies. Some people lived in societies where taxes were paid in goods or services or even used a

---

[66] Waris (2008)
[67] Buttner (1970) p. 276

form of currency, and others had little experience with monetary and taxation systems. During colonisation, the decision to introduce a capitalist economy, in order to send raw materials back to the imperial state from a predominantly African communal or socialist society, led to the introduction of taxes with varying rates depending on the community.[68] Those that opposed colonisation the most paid more hut/poll tax than those quick to collaborate. For example, in Kenya the Kikuyu paid a 2 shillings hut tax, and the Maasai paid 12 shillings in hut tax to the British.[69]

With such varied understanding and experiences at play, how can the state run a fiscal system that works for all without also investing in public education about the system and its evolution – past and future?

Third challenge. States have failed to develop and update fiscal treaties, constitutions, laws, regulations, and policies. Many developing countries still have very old legal documents. Constitutions are newer (i.e. 2010 in Kenya[70] and 2011 in Morocco[71])[72], but the laws surrounding the area of finance tend to be outdated. In Kenya the income tax act in force is the 1920 colonial model ordinance adopted at independence.[73] It has been amended several times, but most of the legislative provisions in it remain substantially the text of the 1920 colonial law.

Finance-related regulations and policies, if existent, are often not implemented or enforced. Kenya, however, developed transfer pricing regulations.[74] Several other countries, including Uganda, South Africa, Morocco and Egypt, have adopted transfer pricing regulations.[75] Transfer pricing regulations are rules guiding how multinational enterprises (MNEs) can move or transfer goods or

---

[68] Waris (2008) p. 286

[69] Waris (2013b)

[70] Republic of Kenya (2010)

[71] Kingdom of Morocco (2011)

[72] For links to many African constitutions, see www.ascleiden.nl/content/webdossiers/african-constitutions

[73] Republic of Kenya (1988)

[74] See Waris (2013a, 2014a, 2017b)

[75] Curtis and Todorova (2012) p. 4

services at cost within the different holdings of the company without attracting taxable profits across multiple countries.

Many treaties are similarly inherited from before independence and, again, need to be revisited, reflected upon, and discarded or reformed. Kenya reviewed treaties after independence, however the actual text of the treaties never changed, possibly because of a failure to understand their economic effects on the country.

Fourth challenge. Most African countries have not been committing financial resources to honour international commitments. Multilateral and bilateral conventions or treaties, state contracts, declarations, resolutions and comments set out the minimum standards to which states agree to be bound. By participating in the international framework, states agree to undertake that constitutions, laws, policies, and budgets reflect these legal obligations and that corresponding policies are applied. However, disclosure of relevant information and the enforcement of these obligations through policy implementation and financing remain within state control. The political will of the state regarding international obligations is clearly reflected from regime to regime in the actions a government takes or fails to take. African countries are party to many texts and have yet to honour them, for example, the Abuja Declaration, signed by all African states, calls states to use a minimum of 15% of their national budgets on healthcare. The African Union target of 1% of GDP invested in research and development has been respected by less than a handful of countries.[76]

Fifth challenge. The challenge of the separation of state from business continues to overwhelm the running of the government and the potential of the economy. On average in developing countries, 80% of the economy tends to be through government business and public procurement. Many African countries followed the example of Kenya where, between 1970 and 2000, civil servants could own businesses. These civil servants will be retiring in the next 5 to 10 years, by 2030. Over that period of 30 years, many civil servants in government secured procurement tenders for their private

---

[76] UNESCO (2018)

companies and for those within their networks (families and close friends as well as tribe members).

This continues to undermine the stability of the economy; tenders are opaque due to the absence of registers of beneficial ownership, and this leaves a wide margin for the perception and potential of corruption.[77] The law has been amended, and newly recruited civil servants are no longer allowed to hold additional jobs, but many government employees remain in this dilemma.

In Guinea, however, government officials are not allowed to have other businesses or jobs running simultaneously. A 2015 analysis of the landscape of government procurement in sub-Saharan Africa found that African countries like Namibia, Botswana, Angola and South Africa are still grappling with inefficiencies in public procurement, despite there being robust legal and institutional frameworks in place.[78]

Sixth challenge. The issue of corruption continues to undermine the ability of the state to collect taxes. In South Africa, after the allegations of state capture during the Zuma government, the public procurement sector was exposed as prone to corruption, with the 2018 South Africa Corruption Report detailing the preferential treatment accorded to black elites at the expense of others.[79] A scandal in Kenya, showing procurement contracts where towels were being purchased by the National Youth Service for 1,000 Euros each, further undermined the willingness of taxpayers to contribute to the state. Although the government arrested people involved in the theft of approximately 500,000 Euros, 8.5 million Euros remain unaccounted for, and the people responsible have not been arrested.[80] Evidence of good spending develops taxpayer compliance more effectively than efficient systems and well trained staff.

Seventh challenge. While there has been an impetus to train revenue authority staff in African countries on issues of taxation, there have been no similar trainings for staff at ministries of finance, the national treasury, the attorney general's office, or the judiciary. Nor is their

---

[77] Nsehe (2015)
[78] Ernst and Young (2015)
[79] GAN Business Anti-Corruption Portal (2018)
[80] *The Star* (2018)

training in financial and fiscal matters for the general public. The result is that the better capacitated revenue officials are perceived as being more knowledgeable but also more aggressive than before. In addition, when disputes need to go for resolution, the decisions can be swayed if a judge has limited knowledge about tax claims and tax matters more generally. In addition, international organizations and private companies have a bias for their own regulations and models. For example, the OECD and accounting firms favour training that makes their work and the work of their clients easier. They thus have a bias towards training with an eye to achieving their own ends.

Eighth challenge. Lack of clarity on matters of the state in relation to domestic affairs and other states makes for poor domestic, regional and continental tax and fiscal planning and policy. Kenya on the one hand ranked prominently in the 2018 Financial Secrecy Index (FSI) and on the other has passed legislation to set up the Nairobi International Financial Centre (NIFC). Other African countries listed in the FSI include Mauritius, Seychelles, South Africa and Botswana.[81] Despite this, the current African membership of the UN Tax Committee includes Kenya, along with Ghana, Djibouti, and Nigeria, with technical support from the African Tax Administration Forum (ATAF).

Another area calling out for more clarity has to do with the taxation of multinational enterprises (MNEs). Many African countries have signed onto the OECD led Multilateral Convention on Mutual Administrative Assistance in Tax Matters. However, it remains unclear what policy position African countries will take on the taxation of MNEs. There seems to be little hesitation to sign onto international platforms and simultaneously little attention to and intentionality about how participation in the platforms could advance matters at domestic levels. These contradictions can erode the trust the public invests in public authorities.

Ninth challenge. Participation in and access of people to the state is limited predominantly to those that lobby. For example, in Kenya, in reviewing the Income Tax Bill of 2018,[82] only eight days were

---

[81] FSI (2018)
[82] Republic of Kenya (2018)

accorded for comments, and the people receiving publicity on their opinions in the national media seem to be accounting firms and other big private companies.

Lack of public participation in legislative processes leads to skewed understandings by people and politicians of issues and can result in the passing of laws that are not holistic or well thought through. Similarly, the draft Finance Bill was released, again with an eight-day window for comment accorded by the Cabinet Secretary of Finance. The short delay potentially contravenes the constitutionally guaranteed requirement of public participation, but the state has failed to create laws regarding public participation or contravention of the implementation of the constitution. In many African countries, the windows for participation in law-making processes may be longer or even shorter, however there is growing thirst among people to make democracies work by participating in them. The learning curve will be high for the public and for governments.

Tenth challenge. The network of wealth chains globally and the secrecy jurisdictions in which their nodes sit allow for the continual holding of assets in foreign states to which developing country tax collectors have no access for information on transfers made.[83] Residents and non-residents continue to place their assets and accounts and companies in certain countries to evade and avoid taxes. The use of technology to enable foreign transactions acerbates this problem.

This challenge comes last, but it is probably one of the biggest facing any country. Removing secrecy provisions and sharing all information regarding domestic taxpayers is very important. Domestic resource mobilisation depends on appropriate rules for the global fiscal architecture and how it operates in an ever evolving technologically enabled world.

Unfortunately, the lack of societal capacity in African countries to understand the system upon self-rule has led to the failure of the African governments to adequately address this and the other challenges over the years. This results in the ongoing undermining of the fiscal legitimacy of the state. The refusal of government officials

---

[83] Seabrooke and Wigan (2017) p. 22

to pay taxes also undermines the entire fabric of the fiscal legitimacy of the state. It is possible, however, through analysis and dialogue to develop solutions for the challenges and indicators of an improved system that helps build the state and serve the people.

In Lesotho, the Sotho say, "The child of the crab walks sideways like its mother." Africa is a product of its history, background and experiences, and it too is walking sideways. However, perhaps if we consider carefully the houses we need and look carefully at the available timbers, we will build states that better serve Africans. If we strengthen the legs of the horse, we might slow down, but we will not fail. The well will never dry, if we are attentive, and bold.

1.4. Building African states

> *In the moment of crisis, the wise build bridges*
> *and the foolish build dams.*
>
> Proverb from Nigeria

Africa is moving towards bridge-building via AfCFTA. Though tax regimes are varied and often without clear principles, rules, guidelines and limitations, there are moves towards greater coherence and harmonisation. Lack of legal and regulatory clarity is unjustifiable in any country and needs to be contained, especially considering poor fiscal legitimacy and global economic instability.

A critical analysis of the power African governments wield in the collection and distribution of taxes is well overdue. The argument in this section is that governments do not have an automatic ability to collect resources and that the failure of states to provide commensurate goods and services means that the right of government to levy charges on the pretext that some form of (additional) service is being accorded is a fallacy that needs to be overturned.

States and societies should determine the compliance of fiscal systems adopted by their countries with internationally recognised standards of state budgeting, with specific reference to how African countries collect revenue and tax residents. Based on those findings, they should propose how best to legislate, and to develop and implement policy, to ensure that appropriate constitutional provisions exist and are enacted. At a microlevel within a democratic society, the budget and government expenditures of public money should reflect the wants, needs and hopes of the people.

This book investigates how taxes and other state revenues are collected and expended. The intent is to make it easier for people to understand and find their way through tax and fiscal systems in Africa. It is written for those interested in state building and in the development of the continent. It is written for those with legal, business, and economic interests. It is written for those interested in the wellbeing of the people of the continent.

The discussions draw on the economic principles of Smith, Ricardo, and Ibn Khaldun and on theories of fiscal sociology of Schumpeter, while keeping an eye on the SDGs. It explores tax principles, critiques current systems, and suggests improvements, drawing on African philosophies, to achieve a fiscally legitimate state. For those interested in more theory, in linkages between tax and human rights, or in the historical development of Kenya's tax system, this book can be read together with *Tax and Development: Solving Kenya's Fiscal Crisis through Human Rights.*[84]

Tax landscapes – at global, continental, regional, national, county/state levels, and community levels – require greater consistency. Government revenue has become a risk. It is time to reconsider the business model. Greater expertise, transparency, and information sharing will have positive business and institutional impacts. Taxpayers and other stakeholders in African states need understanding to strategize, engage in scenario planning, and reform systems. They need tools to help decide on priority areas of concern and align public investments with public interests, for the long-term stability of African societies.

1.5. Introduction to subsequent chapters

Chapter 1 introduced fiscal law and policy and described the context of the African continent from which examples will be drawn

---

[84] Waris (2013a)

throughout the book. Chapter 2 unpacks theories of the fiscal state and of fiscal legitimacy and sets out the challenges and indicators of fiscal law and policy. Chapter 3 looks at different types of fiscal systems and how they are financed. Chapter 4 discusses budgets and the principles guiding the creation of budgets. Chapter 5 analyses the stakeholders in a fiscal system. Chapter 6 makes recommendations, and Chapter 7 concludes.

Peace is costly but it is worth the expense.

Proverb from Kenya

Chapter 2

The Unfolding Theory of the Fiscal State

Your neighbour knows you are alive,
but only you know how you are living.

Oromo proverb

General societal compliance to law is a direct reflection of the legitimacy of a state, and by extension, tax compliance reflects the fiscal legitimacy of a state.[85] The guiding principles of a fiscal state begin with the trust society has in its leaders, which trust grants the leaders their legitimacy.[86] This leads to compliance by members of a society to the fiscal laws of the state. Fiscal legitimacy is made up of several key principles: accountability, responsibility, transparency (the three good governance principles), effectiveness, efficiency, fairness, and justice.[87]

States can enhance fiscal legitimacy. First, they should involve independent third parties in auditing and evaluating public policies, to strengthen transparency and accountability.[88] Second, they should promote better, fairer and more public spending. Third, they should broaden the tax base and make tax systems fairer and more balanced.[89] Finally, they could reinforce the capacity, authority and accountability of continental, regional, national and subnational government bodies.

Strengthening administrative capabilities and promoting societal participation[90] and open and informed debate result in more transparency.[91] Independent actors with the capacity and financial

---

[85] Waris (2018a)

[86] Waris (2013b)

[87] Waris and Latif (2015)

[88] Waris (2013a) p. 155

[89] Waris (2013b)

[90] Participation in budgetary planning has grown globally. In 1999, about 40,000 residents of Porto Alegre, Brazil participated in public meetings to allocate about half the city's annual budget. In 2018, the governor of Makueni county in Kenya began participatory audits of spending in the county.

[91] Waris (2013c)

independence to carry out the critical evaluation of policies and proposed reforms can also add to good governance and fiscal legitimacy. Achieving a fiscally legitimate system is always a compromise and will always be suboptimal.[92] Nonetheless, a state and its society need to continually and consistently work towards the principles of fiscal legitimacy. Two of the principles, according to the thinking of Ibn Khaldun, should never be compromised: fairness and justice.[93] These principles allow "you to know how you are living." In relating the fiscal principles of fairness and justice to the Oromo proverb, they encourage a spirit of unpacking measures to check on one's own state and the state of neighbours and of benchmarking, comparing, and enhancing equity among people in society.

This chapter will engage with the seven principles set out above and explore how they are implemented in the developed and developing worlds, with a focus on the fiscal, and specifically tax, systems of African countries. A historical analysis using the lenses of fiscal sociology and the fiscal state and a human rights approach to social welfare spending was carried out in *Tax and Development*.[94] This book builds on that theoretical framework to holistically analyse African countries' current fiscal systems.

2.1. Principles of fiscal legitimacy

Africa and its regions, states, societies and fiscal systems are inextricably intertwined. Interconnectivity is expressed in the fiscal bargain between the state and society, which bargain grants the state the fiscal legitimacy to collect and distribute revenue. Fiscal legitimacy is based on the confidence that a society has in the governance of the fiscal state.[95] The ability of the state to take loans, do business, and collect resource rents is fairly stable, however, the tax bargain negotiated between the state and society is constantly changing and is reflected in the laws and policies that govern the levy and distribution of taxes. Even if people are less aware of the

---

[92] Waris and Latif (2015)
[93] Waris (2015)
[94] Waris (2013a)
[95] Waris (2019)

resources government absorbs from businesses, loans and natural resource rents[96], if the evolving tax bargain is perceived by society as fair and just, the fiscal legitimacy of the state is maintained and a fiscal crisis is averted.

Almost every country in the world prepares its budget using principles and canons of taxation to achieve fiscal legitimacy. The state decides what tax to collect, from whom to collect, in what amount, to whom to grant exemptions, and whether it is fair or economically feasible to collect.[97] There seems to be less clarity around resources from business, debt, and rent, however. The state budget in most African countries is prepared by a group made up predominantly of economists in ministries of finance and/or planning. They compromise on issues, usually to collect the most from the wealthy, using principles of progressive tax systems, before presenting the budget in parliament. There are also political compromises, depending on the strength of lobbyists, and the result is always suboptimal.

Although this description makes budget preparation sound like a simple, well-organized and fairly straightforward process, it is a highly politicized, complex and convoluted process, with little clarity until the final compromise is reached. Despite the complex negotiations and trade-offs, compromise-based budgets reflect fiscal principles, because choices must be justified at the legal, economic, social and political levels. In this real world of fiscal decision-making, principles allow for the most rational compromise possible based on guiding principles. However, which set of principles, economic thinking and general fiscal philosophy a state relies on varies and these impact upon development of the fiscal state. Unfortunately, only 26 out of the 54 African countries have been analysed for the implementation of the SDGs and ensured that commitments on alleviating poverty are used in this process.[98]

---

[96] Resource rent is the profit or remainder of the sales price after all costs and normal returns have been deducted from sale of the mineral, oil or gas. Arnason (2008)

[97] The approach of asking as many questions as possible using the 5Ws and 1H: who, what, when, where, why and how.

[98] United Nations (2019)

This book argues that for the state, which is responsible to those who entrust it with their limited resources for the wellbeing of society, fiscal legitimacy is critical and is attained through the accountability, responsibility, transparency, efficiency, effectiveness, fairness and justness of its fiscal system. The interplay between limited resources and their distribution – at the discretion of fiscal states based on their spending priorities – has resulted in development, poverty alleviation, and the improvement of the lifestyles of people in some states.

State-society relations are complex and different for different groups of people. The types of relationships between citizens and developed states, through state mechanisms and institutions, have not been as successful in improving the lives of citizens in post-colonial and post-conflict developing states. In such states, which are the focus of this book, collection needs to be improved and spending priorities reviewed, especially in the context of the global financial crisis, with greater resource constraints. The state's fiscal legitimacy and societal interactions are lenses through which to look to know where there is need for reform.

2.2. Indicators of a fiscally legitimate state

The lead cow (the one in front) gets whipped the most.

Zulu proverb

Different countries grow and develop differently. Countries can nonetheless be categorized, so that an analyst would know what type of state one is dealing with. To categorize, we can look into the following aspects of the state: financial theory, form of government, central administration, local administration, officeholders, state responsibilities, method of financing, public finance, expenditure, revenues, credit structure, the role of the economy, economic policy, public enterprises, political participation, social consequences, statistics and finally the causes of instability.

Variations in financial theories and forms of government and other areas lead to inevitable uniqueness, so on the one hand, it can be difficult to categorize sates clearly and precisely. On the other, the various ways in which states combine diverse approaches leads to possible categorizations. Ormrod, Bonney and Bonney[99] developed a model to do just that, which includes indicators such as those mentioned above, i.e. economic policy and political participation. The model was elaborated upon by Waris who added the indicators of human rights[100] and fiscal literacy[101] and von Kommer and Waris[102] who added the indicator of tax administration. The adapted Ormrod and Bonney model of the developmental stages of the fiscal state is shared in a table in Appendix B. It categorizes states as tribute state, domain state, tax state, and fiscal state.

Stronger economies in a region or continent receive the brunt of competition and challenge and are tested more on issues around corruption and proper accountability, a reflection of the Zulu proverb about the head cow getting whipped the most.

African states are a mix of tribute, domain and tax states, with elements of a fiscal state through diverse forms of social welfare provisions, but this continually shifts based on policies of the government in power. The Ormrod and Bonney model, however informative, remains incomplete because it does not consider states in a globalised world with a plethora of interactions within and between states, regions, and continents. Its second weakness is its failure to address the colonial state and the effects the imperial and former imperial state continue to have on the fiscal development of a state. A final gap is consideration of the constitutionality of the financing of the state. What should the political regime's power be regarding tax, and how should parliament and its oversight play a greater role, together with constitutional provisions to support the state?

Fiscal and tax law draw on economics and society and politics. This chapter will delve into the economic principles that guide the making of fiscal and tax law. It will describe state resources including taxation and the general principles and canons guiding taxation. It will as well discuss several other instruments of a fiscal system:

---

[99] Ormrod, Bonney and Bonney (1999)
[100] Waris (2013a)
[101] Waris (2014c); Waris and Murangwa (2012)
[102] Von Kommer and Waris (2013)

taxation, debt and loans, intergovernmental aid, other sources of government revenue, and expenditure.

2.2.1. Taxation

Bellies mixed up, crocodiles mixed up,
we have between us only one belly, but if we get anything to eat
it passes down our respective gullets.

Ashanti proverb

There are many diverse understandings and definitions of tax. This section discusses diverse definitions, pointing to the differences and, depending on which definition is selected, the effects from a theoretical and practical point of view on a state.

Globally, the definition of tax is contested. Scholars, institutions, lawmakers, and society have attempted to define it. They take taxation on from the summation of their experiences, context and understandings. The question arises, therefore, of whether it is possible to have one definition of taxation and whether that is necessary. If we were to try to come to an understanding of a definition of what taxation is, what would that look like, and is there an African understanding that makes sense for African societies? Would the definition be the same between developed and developing countries or even between different states at different levels of development?

Scholars like Dalton[103] Taussig[104] and Seligman[105] define tax as a compulsory contribution imposed by a public authority, irrespective of the exact amount of service rendered to the taxpayer in return and without reference to special benefits conferred to defray the common costs of the society. Judges have also tried to define tax, for example Chief Justice (CJ) Latham in the United Kingdom (UK) case of **Matthews v Chicory Board**.[106] The Chief Justice termed tax as a compulsory exaction of money by a public authority for public

---

[103] Dalton (2009)
[104] Taussig (1911)
[105] Seligman (1908)
[106] [1938] 60 Common Law Reports (CLR) 263

purposes, enforceable by law, and which is not a payment for services rendered. Practitioners through the OECD have a working definition of taxes as "compulsory, unrequited payments to general government."[107]

In summary, a tax from a European lens is a compulsory levy imposed by a government on persons residing within its jurisdiction. The government may use this revenue to provide social services and amenities for the benefit of all. There is no obligation on the part of the government to provide any specific services for the tax payments received.[108] There is no corresponding entitlement to receive a *quid pro quo* from the government.[109] It is not a price paid by the taxpayer for any definite service rendered or commodities supplied by the government. The benefits received by taxpayers from the government are not based on them being taxpayers. A tax is a generalised exaction, which may be levied on one or more criteria upon individuals, groups of individuals, or other legal entities. With this definition one could argue that there is a weak if almost non-existent fiscal social contract.

This position, held predominantly by northern scholars, was employed by imperial states vis-à-vis their colonies around the world to ensure that money for taxes could be continually collected, without challenge. This definition was reinforced and further supported to prevent the occupants of the colonies from demanding that taxes collected be spent on the people in the geographical region from where they were collected.[110] For example, tax payments from Brazil were used to rebuild Lisbon after the war. Tax payments were collected for over 100 years, even after Lisbon had been rebuilt. In most colonies, including in Africa, such taxation practices, with the realisation of their oppressive nature, led to calls for independence.[111]

Brennan and Buchanan,[112] political scientist and economist, argue that the power to tax does not carry with it the obligation to use tax

---

[107] OECD (1996) p. 3
[108] OECD (1996) p. 4
[109] Quid pro quo means something given or taken as an equivalent.
[110] Waris (2007)
[111] Waris (2013a)
[112] Brennan and Buchanan (1980) pp. 8-9

revenue in a particular way. It is simply a power to take. As a result, all constitutional rules may be limiting the power to tax. Brennan and Buchanan state that there is no commensurate right of citizenry for the money they remit to government. It could be argued, though, that no one may be deprived of property arbitrarily, and thus there is an entitlement for that deprivation. However, the power to tax debate does not make room for this argument. This debate of power versus right to tax must look at the constitutionality of taxation and provisions for finance found within constitutions to trace the legitimacy of the state to collect taxes.

The principle of John Locke, echoed by the French philosophers of the 18th century, is that man is entitled to the fruits of his labour.[113] Locke thus concluded that it is a contradiction in a free society for government to take more than half the fruits of a man's labour. In the 18th century, progressive thinkers such as Locke[114] and Hume[115] felt taxation was wrong. Arguments that dispose of the fairness concept usually argue for security and defence. Defence is seen as being more important than opulence[116], and many allow the imposition of tariffs to prevent dependence on imports.[117] Malthus also supported the concept of high tariffs, based on the argument of potential future wars, agreeing with Adam Smith.[118] Ricardo, however, disagreed with this analysis and felt that no matter what sanctions were imposed, food would always be allowed through.[119]

African philosophers on tax are few, but Ibn Khaldun's argument of fairness remains the most important, where he argued that taxes should be kept at a minimum.[120] In the modern era, for example in exercising power, the revenue authority must exercise fairness in tax assessment. In the 2016 Kenyan case of **Silver Chain Limited v Commissioner Income Tax & 3 others**[121] the court was of the

---

[113] Locke (1690) chapter 5 section 27
[114] Locke (1690)
[115] Hume (1748)
[116] Smith (1977/1776)
[117] Olson (1963) pp. 3-4
[118] Malthus (1814)
[119] Ricardo and Sraffa (1962)
[120] Khaldun (1377)
[121] [2016] eKLR

view that disputes involving tax assessment should be dealt with under the legal procedures set up by the law. In this case, the High Court found the tax assessment oppressive, because the taxpayer was not accorded the right to fair administrative action.

The South African Case of **Anil Singh v Commissioner for the South African Revenue Service**[122] is also illustrative of the fairness approach in taxation. The Supreme Court reiterated that the Commissioner's exercise of power is dependent on the provisions of law, and the act of excluding the notice of assessment was a deprivation of the taxpayer's rights under the law.

The first constitution to address the issue of specific requirements for resources was the French Declaration of 1789. It recognised the transfer of the responsibility for security to the state in exchange for money in its articles 13 and 14:

> 13. A common **contribution** is essential **for** the **maintenance** of the **public forces** and for the cost of **administration.** This should be equitably distributed among all the citizens in proportion to their means.
> 14. **All the citizens have a right to** decide, either personally or by their representatives, as to the necessity of the public contribution; to grant this freely; to know to what uses it is put; and to **fix the proportion, the mode of assessment and of collection and the duration of the taxes.**[123]

Following from this, the constitution of the Republic of France 1793 declared:

> Society owes subsistence to its unfortunate citizens either by giving them work or assuring them the means to exist if they are incapable of work.[124]

According to the Ashanti proverb above, we have a shared belly, and all must partake. State resources play a key role in helping countries reach the SDGs. Governments seek to use taxation to finance their social and physical infrastructure needs, provide a stable and predictable fiscal environment to promote economic growth and investment, promote good governance and accountability by

---

[122] [2003 Mar 31] Supreme Court of Appeal of South Africa ZASCA

[123] Republic of France (1789)

[124] Republic of France (1793)

strengthening the relationship between government and citizens, and ensure that the costs and benefits of development are fairly shared.[125]

Before colonization, societies in Africa had a taxation system that served different purposes. Land was communally owned, and members of a community accessed land by virtue of being a member of that community.[126] Once harvesting had been done, each member gave the chief or the council of elders a portion of what they had harvested. This was used to feed the chief and his family who administered the community and the warrior clan which provided security to members of the community. Tax was also paid so that a traveller would be granted safe passage through the lands of a community. Arabs at the Indian Ocean coast applied a tax system based on Islamic religious principles. Taxes were mainly voluntary and were used, in addition to administration, to assist the poor and support individuals serving Islam.[127]

Fiscal systems can play a key role in both furthering democratic representation and ensuring higher standards of living and wellbeing through wealth and employment creation in the country. It is in this light that we talk of fiscal systems, not just in the technical sense of simply raising revenues, but rather in terms of social development. Before a state can protect its citizens, it needs to raise money to finance the governance structures required. Through its key role as the tie that binds the ruler and the ruled, taxation supports representation, accountability and state capacity.[128]

In some African countries, like Kenya, taxation is the single largest source of government budgetary resources. Taxation has been applied to meet the following objectives. First, it raises revenue to fund public spending without recourse to excessive public sector borrowing and mobilizes revenue in ways that are equitable and that minimize its disincentive effects on economic activities.[129] Second, taxation promotes social welfare by putting a check on the consumption of commodities regarded as harmful and discouraging

---

[125] Pfister (2009) p. 6
[126] Waris (2007)
[127] Waris (2013a)
[128] Waris, Kohonen, Ranguma and Mosioma (2009)
[129] Moyi and Ronge (2006)

the consumption of goods and services with high social costs or demerit goods.[130] It is for this reason that spirits, alcohol, and tobacco are heavily taxed.

Third, taxation serves as a protection policy to protect indigenous industries from the effects of cheap imported goods. For example, sugar and rice from non-COMESA countries are highly taxed to make the prices of such imports higher than locally produced sugar and rice. However, with the advent of the AfCFTA, this will change. Fourth, taxation redistributes income to reduce inequalities of incomes. When ability to pay is taken into consideration, the government can use taxation to distribute income more or less equally among all those who benefit from government.

Finally, taxation contributes to economic stability and influences the level of aggregate demand in the economy. These eventually affect the level of economic growth in the country. For example, taxes such as VAT have a direct impact on the consumption of goods and services, because higher taxes may lead to higher prices and hence lower consumption levels. The Kenyan constitution, for instance, in reference to the utilisation of public funds, stipulates that "expenditure shall promote the equitable development of the country, including by making special provision for marginalized groups and areas."[131]

Taxes are not to be used for the follow reasons. First, taxes should not be used to coerce individuals to enter the labour force and work as was the case in the Hut and Poll tax introduced by the colonialists that failed to obey the principles of taxation.[132] Second, taxes are not to be used to support bloated, corrupt and inefficient governments. The Kenyan constitution for example states that "public money shall be used in a prudent and responsible way."[133] The principle of productivity, also known as the principle of fiscal

---

[130] In economics, a demerit good "is defined as a good which can have a negative impact on the consumer – but these damaging effects may be unknown or ignored by the consumer. Demerit goods also usually have negative externalities – where consumption causes a harmful effect on a third party."
www.economicshelp.org/blog/glossary/demerit-goods

[131] Republic of Kenya (2010) article 201 (b) (iii)

[132] Waris (2007)

[133] Republic of Kenya (2010) article 201 (d)

adequacy, requires authorities to raise sufficient revenue for the government, such that there should be no need to resort to deficit financing.[134]

Finally, taxes are not to be used to further individual interests as seen, for example, in the attempt of the 2017-2022 Kenyan Parliament to increase their retirement package at the expense of public interest. Global as well as continental reports show that MNEs and African political leaders avoid and evade tax in their countries, and most of them maintain offshore accounts and property in other jurisdictions, hence, through tax evasion, depriving their countries of much needed resources.[135] The political and business elite should not be able to use their power to satisfy selfish interests.[136]

Tax is necessary to finance the activities of the state. There have been debates as to whether the government is efficient in the provision of social services, like education, and if the private sector would do a better job. However, some research shows there is no real difference in efficiency based on who administers revenue spending; the difference is rather in who benefits from new business.[137] Scholars agree that authorities have a responsibility to ensure that taxes are just.[138] First, they must be collected for a purpose that is not immoral. Second, they must be used to feed the hungry, house the homeless or clothe the poor.[139] Third, they must be imposed by a legitimate legislative authority. Fourth, they must be levied for a just cause. Finally, the tax burden must be equitably shared.[140]

Article 35 of the 2011 constitution of the Kingdom of Morocco[141] protects the right to hold private property, but the law may limit the exercise of this right in favour of the economic and social development of the country. Article 39 of the Moroccan constitution creates a duty to pay taxes in proportion to capacity (ability to pay principle), and only the law may create public

---

[134] Waris (2007)
[135] Kvamme (2017)
[136] Muthoni (2017)
[137] Akech (2006)
[138] McGee (2011)
[139] McGee (2011)
[140] Waris (2007)
[141] Kingdom of Morocco (2011)

expenditures. According to article 71 of the 2011 Moroccan constitution, the parliament has the competence to create laws regarding the fiscal regime, the tax basis, and the modalities of tax collection. Article 77 of the constitution gives Government the ability to oppose law reform when it has an impact on public expenditures. However, the Moroccan constitution doesn't provide instruments to protect the taxpayer; the "tax principles" are a function of public expenditure and broaden the power of the state. The Moroccan constitution does not set quality standards for interpreting or applying tax law. However, the 2011 constitution does create institutions and legal procedures, and there is a move towards more public participation.

In some traditional African societies, the chief/king/queen/ruler was supported through diverse forms of payment including but not limited to food, voluntary service, fulfilment of periodic and specific activity as well as money depending on the level of development of the community. Excesses were not taken, and the state was financed based on need. Oppressive rulers were soon deposed and often, societies operated direct and not representative democracy. This traditional system still exists in the minds and operates within societies in both urban and rural areas on the African continent. African communalism and African socialism are both concepts very similar to those of the welfare state. Thus, this book will move forward with the French constitutional understanding of taxation, based on the premise that resources are for a reason.

2.2.2. Debt and loans

Fiscal space is the difference between a country's debt limit[142] and the current debt level. Constrained fiscal space reflects, to varying degrees, the high financing risks from financial markets and relatively high levels of financing needs and debt servicing needs in the continent. Even though the degree of strain varies across the African continent, countries with a highly constrained fiscal space run into

---

[142] The debt limit approach to estimating fiscal space assumes that governments only borrow as a last resort (i.e. after exhausting all the financing options available).

financial market access risks, which can impair their ability to effectively use fiscal policy for economic and social development. African governments should therefore make it a priority to build adequate fiscal space and use it judiciously, without impairing the long-term economic health of the country. The IMF argues for fiscal consolidation not only in countries with limited fiscal space, but also in countries with some or substantial fiscal space. This is because, even if an economy is in a relatively strong position, there is always need to build buffers based on risks on the horizon.

Governments should only use fiscal space when there is an existing strong case justifying its utilization. In Africa, the need to finance SDGs justifies the call for building and utilizing fiscal space. Policy makers must strive not only to build fiscal space, but also to leverage public-private sector partnerships to achieve some of the SDG targets. Additionally, creating fiscal space requires governments to thoroughly scrutinize all public spending, to ensure it is not only directed towards improving productivity but also aligned to the achievement of the SDGs, either directly as drivers or indirectly as enablers.

The International Financial Institution Advisory Commission has noted that the "use of IMF resources and conditionality to control the economies of developing nations often undermines the sovereignty and democratic processes of member governments receiving assistance."[143] In an attempt to ensure sound financial footing for its local governments created in 1976, the Nigerian Federal Government decided to write off all outstanding debts of the local governments owed to the state government.

In 1981, the Nigerian federal government introduced a formula for sharing the federal revenue amongst the three levels of the government. The statutory allocations to the local governments have been witnessing several upward reviews from 10% in 1981 to 20.6% in 2002. During these adjustments, both state and federal government allocations from the federation accounts witnessed some significant drops.[144] Debt levels have not reached pre-HIPC

---

[143] Meltzer (2000)
[144] Ajayi (1991); Tiffen, Mortimore and Gichuki (1994)

levels, and the risk of debt distress is still low or moderate in most African countries. But debt accumulation remains a threat, given that debt-to-GDP ratios remain above 50% in some countries (such as Gambia, Mauritania, São Tomé and Príncipe, and Uganda).

Tanzania's public debt increased in recent years and is relatively high compared to the average for the East African Community region or the median for sub-Sahara African and low-income countries. As of December 2016, for example, public debt amounted to 24 billion USD compared to the actual tax revenue of the first half of fiscal year 2016-2017, which was only about 3.12 billion USD. However, economists argue that the debt seems to be sustainable.[145]

Fiscal policy seems to have ambiguous effects on inclusive growth and on inequalities in Africa. Africa's high debt levels pose a concern to the continent's long-term growth and development. The rise in government debt and the vulnerability of fiscal policy in Africa have exposed governments on the margins of solvency to debt difficulties. African governments need policy frameworks that promote stable income and expenditure flows. Wherever possible, governments should finance their deficits through domestic currency markets by issuing financial obligations with the longest possible maturity.

2.2.3. Aid

External revenues are comprised of loans and aid. The continent has the following partners for its external aid revenues: The World Bank, the European Union, the African Development Bank (AfDB), the Islamic Development Bank, and the International Monetary Fund (IMF). Aid is used to help build up a tax system. The education and capacity of the revenue authority were weaknesses observed among tax offices and authorities. The focus of aid went to answer the need to build up the revenue authority.[146] A lot of donor aid money goes into education for and capacity building of revenue authority officials. However, aid money is not going to help people

---

[145] Republic of Tanzania (2017b); World Bank (2017b) pp. 11-12; World Bank (2017c)
[146] OECD (2014)

understand why they even pay taxes or what other revenue government obtains and how it is spent.

2.2.4. Other government revenue

Other government revenue includes income from property; shareholding dividends; sales of goods and services; fines, penalties and forfeits; and miscellaneous and unidentified revenue. Grants are:

> transfers receivable by government units, from other resident or nonresident government units or international organizations, […] without receiving from the latter any good, service, or asset in return as a direct counterpart. Grants are normally receivable in cash, but may also take the form of the receipt of goods or services (in kind).[147]

Property income covers revenues obtained as rents or royalties as well as interest, dividends and other income from property. Rents and royalties are income from natural resources leased to private or foreign investors for exploration and extraction. Interest is the revenue from financial assets of the government that are put in other institutions.[148]

Dividends are the revenue earned on shareholding by government through investments in corporations and profit withdrawal from state-owned enterprises (SOEs). Sales of goods and services are sales by market establishments (such as rental of government buildings and equipment); administrative fees for services (i.e. fees for drivers' licences, passports, visas; court fees; fees for birth, marriage or death certificates; patent registrations); and sales by nonmarket establishments such as fees at government hospitals, tuition fees at government schools, and admission fees to museums and parks. Fines, penalties and forfeits are compulsory transfers imposed:

> by courts of law or quasijudicial bodies for violations of laws or administrative rules. Out-of-court agreements are also included. Forfeits are amounts that were deposited with a general government unit pending a legal or administrative proceeding and that have been transferred to the general government unit as part of the resolution of that proceeding.[149]

---

[147] IMF (2014) pp. 103-104
[148] IMF (2014) chapter 5
[149] IMF (2014) p. 111

Miscellaneous and unidentified revenue includes donations from individuals, private non-profit organizations, and nongovernmental foundations and corporations; compensations for damages not covered by insurance policies; and unclaimed estates.

In some countries, it is not straightforward to identify these sources of revenue. One needs to be aware of country-specific nuances with regards to the classification of some taxes and non-tax revenue, depending on the nature for which the revenue collection is made. For instance, Benin collects an overnight stay tax, a forest products tax, a tax on mobile operators, a tax on boats, and revenues from public administrations.[150] Even if these revenues are identified as taxes, they are levied as regulatory fees. Mauritius introduced environmental protection fees levied on mobile phones, batteries for motor vehicles, and pneumatic tyres, as a fiscal instrument to boost government coffers.[151] Mauritius also has passenger fees, passenger solidarity fees,[152] a special levy on banks, a special levy on telecommunications companies, and advertising structure fees.[153]

Public receipts that are not considered taxes include monies charged for the provision of specific goods and services; special assessments such as the levies on certain members of the community who are beneficiaries of certain government activities related to public projects; fines such as court fines; fees for registering marriages, births and deaths; profits from paper currency and mintage; and deficit financing.[154] For the payment to be extracted, the service must be given, for example, as was decided in the 1999

---

[150] African Development Bank (2018a) p. 122

[151] Republic of Mauritius (2002) Part X

[152] This is a tax on carbon dioxide emissions similar to a carbon tax but deposited in UNITAID spent specifically on climate change. Other countries that levy this tax include Cameroon, Chile, Congo, France, Madagascar, Mali, Mauritius, Niger and the Republic of Korea.

[153] Republic of Mauritius (2007) p. 17

[154] Deficit financing means excess of public expenditure over public revenue. The excess is met by borrowings from the market abroad or creation of currency. Presently in Kenya, the judiciary has policy to make itself financially independent. Although this is a laudable principle, what happens to the profit and thus the moral or ethical question: Should justice be a profitable business?

Kenyan case of **Karen and Langata Residents Association v The City Council of Nairobi and Another**:

> that granted an order of mandamus to compel the Minister for Local Government to direct the City Council to perform the duties imposed upon it by the Local Government Act for the benefit of the applicant and for purposes of proper accountability to the electorate in the applicant's area.[155]

Kenya's other government revenue includes property income; business permits; social security contributions; fines; penalties and forfeitures; and interest and other income from lending.[156] Other countries report other types of government revenue.

Benin imposed fees for utilization of roads, charges on electronic communications, and royalty payments by a mobile operator.[157] Chad charges for motor vehicles have just been abolished and replaced by a "special tax on petroleum products" of approximately 50 US cents per litre. Chad's flight boarding charge was abolished in 2016, and instead an "airport modernization" fee was introduced, about approximately USD 17 for an economy class ticket, and approximately USD 25 for an intermediate or business class ticket. An excise duty of 18% was introduced on the turnover generated by the mobile operators, as well as a fee of 50 US cents per minute on every incoming international call. Finally, a levy of 0.2% on imports was introduced to finance the African Union.[158]

Government revenue also includes resources related to unearned mining and forest income or royalties (e.g. timber sales by the Government of Cameroon), dividends distributed by SOEs, and user fees charged against the provision of public services, for example in the form of road and bridge tolls.[159] Road tolls could fill the financing gap for infrastructure in the same way user charges for health and education can be used to allocate important budgets to improve healthcare and the provision of good quality education.[160] However,

---

[155] Karen and Langata Residents Association v The City Council of Nairobi and Another [1999] eKLR
[156] ICPAK (2016)
[157] UNECA (2018)
[158] UNECA (2018)
[159] Mourre and Reut (2019); Bird and Zolt (2003)
[160] Bird and Zolt (2003)

earmarking budgets in this manner or allowing citizens to make out-of-pocket payments like this also creates a loophole for corruption when there is inadequate accountability on the use of the already existing and collected resources.

In addition to corporate taxes, governments collect non-tax revenue from foreign companies extracting natural resources. These can include different types of royalties and levies such as profit sharing, payment for exploration and extraction/investment rights, and natural resource rents paid legally to governments. These also include renewal fees for permits and licenses.

User charges and other fees are important subsets of government revenue and can be paid as water tariffs, electricity bills, fees for telecom services, TV license fees, car license fees, visa fees, license fees for restaurants and bars, land lease or ground rent, penalties on tax arrears, traffic fines, parking fees if parking lots are operated by state entities, and so on. In addition, revenue from stolen assets recovery and fines for evasion and money laundering, while traditionally not considered large amounts, is growing as the work and data surrounding IFF deepens.

In Africa, the financial position is to a considerable extent determined not only by resource endowments but also by geography.[161] Governments in small, land-locked, non-resource-intensive economies have a small fiscal base and are particularly dependent on grant aid from abroad. For example, in Rwanda, the government's overall fiscal deficit peaked in 2014 at 14% of GDP. However, taking out grants, it shows a deficit of nearly 12% in that same year.[162] In other words, its fiscal base could only support 88% of government expenditure. According to the IMF, the government of Rwanda plans to reduce this deficit, principally by increasing domestic revenues, rather than reducing capital or current expenditure.[163]

---

[161] Collier (2006)
[162] World Bank (2017a) p. 12
[163] IMF (2019b)

2.2.5. Expenditure

Poverty is slavery.

Proverb from Somalia

The SDGs and Africa's Agenda 2063 place a high premium on inclusive growth and sustainable development. Africa has recorded notable gains towards some social development outcomes since 2000, although the aggregate progress has not been inclusive enough. For example, public expenditure on say social outcomes such as education and health has generally been on the increase,[164] however, aggregate outcome figures show that the progress has not been inclusive. Achieving the SDGs will require unprecedented levels of development spending and investment from African countries. Public spending will be an essential part of this, as will public borrowing from domestic and international markets.[165] However, without policies to ensure fiscal sustainability, African countries risk fiscal crises. Rising levels of public debt, accelerating especially because of the low tax base in most African countries, are a cause for great concern.[166]

African countries will need to make the most of public borrowing as a source of development finance, while balancing this against the need to minimize the risk of debt crisis. This will include good use of domestic debt markets and mobilizing such markets in promoting financial deepening, financial inclusion, and pro-poor growth. It also requires regional cooperation to facilitate capacity building for strengthened public finance management throughout Africa.

Against this backdrop, overall gains in social outcomes could be expanded and sustained if African countries innovatively mobilise fiscal revenues and effectively deploy them to finance sustainable development. Poverty and inequality have been on the decline but with significant variations across regions and countries. Cost-sharing measures with households for education and health services have

---

[164] Roberts (2003)
[165] UNCTAD (2018)
[166] African Development Bank (2018a); see also ATAF, Waris and Magara (2019) dataset

exacerbated inequality in access to public services and contributed to the slow pace of poverty reduction.[167]

The role of fiscal policy to mobilise financial resources and achieve the SDGs is well articulated in the Addis Ababa Action Agenda (AAAA), which came out of the Third International Conference on Financing for Development in 2015.[168] Under six action areas, the AAAA recognised the need to mobilise significant additional domestic public resources, supplemented by international assistance, to realize sustainable development and achieve the sustainable development goals.

Countries are committed to enhancing revenue administration through modernized, progressive tax systems, improved tax policy, and more efficient tax collection. Countries are also committed to improve the fairness, transparency, efficiency, and effectiveness of tax systems, by broadening the tax base and scaling up international tax cooperation. On the expenditure side, the AAAA stressed the need to strengthen national control mechanisms, such as supreme audit institutions, along with other independent oversight institutions, to enhance transparency and equal participation in the budgeting process. The AAAA called for rationalization of inefficient fossil fuel subsidies that encourage wasteful consumption.

Financing is key to the success of the 2030 Agenda, and sound fiscal policies will play a critical role in leveraging the investment needed to eradicate poverty and ensure inclusive growth. Effective fiscal policies can facilitate economic growth and the achievement of several sustainable development goals (SDGs) and specific SDG targets (T)[169] at the global and national level across different sectors, including in some of the following ways.[170]

Goal 1: No poverty. Revenue collection contributes to national treasuries, which finance national development plans towards reducing poverty (T1.1). Effective fiscal policies, which ensure that profits are taxed where activity takes place and profits are earned,

---

[167] Beegle, Christiaensen, Dabalen and Gaddis (2016)
[168] UNDESA (2015)
[169] These goals with targets are part of the 2030 Agenda (United Nations, 2015a)
[170] Based on UNCTAD (2018)

increase revenue collection. Predictable tax rules are also important for cross-border trade, business investment, jobs creation, and growth which enhances revenue collection.

Goal 6: Clean water and sanitation. Some fiscal reforms (e.g. taxes on water abstraction, regulatory levies, subsidies) can be implemented to improve water quality (T6.3), increase water-use efficiency (T6.4), and generate revenues to improve water access (T6.1). In addition, reforming budgetary expenditures (i.e. subsidies, tax exemptions) in other sectors (e.g. agriculture, energy) can increase the effectiveness of water-related public expenditure, supporting SDG6. Quality economic growth is one that is strong, stable, sustainable, increases productivity, and leads to socially desirable outcomes (such as improved standards of living and poverty alleviation).[171]

Goal 7: Affordable and clean energy. Fiscal policies (e.g. energy taxes, carbon pricing mechanisms, incentives for renewables) can generate revenues to improve energy access (T7.1), support renewable energy generation (T7.2), improve energy efficiency (T7.3), and stimulate private investment in energy infrastructure and clean energy technology (T7a). Reforming budgetary expenditure (i.e. subsidies, tax exemptions) in the energy sector can also support the deployment of clean energy, supporting SDG7 but also SDG12.

Goal 8: Decent work and economic growth. Fiscal policies that promote investment and innovation will attract foreign direct investment (FDI), consequently providing opportunities for decent work and innovation, and generating higher levels of economic productivity (T8.2). Fiscal policies can also improve global resource efficiency in consumption and production (T8.4). Moreover, reforming fiscal policies to reduce tax-induced distortion on labour could increase incentives for employment and support full employment (T8.5).

---

[171] Martinez and Mlachila (2013); Mlachila, Tapsoba and Tapsoba (2014)

Goal 9: Industry, innovation, and infrastructure. Fiscal policies can generate resources and create incentives for private investment in research and development for green technologies, support infrastructure upgrades, and stimulate adoption of clean and environmentally sound technologies and industrial processes (T9.4).

Goal 10: Reduced inequalities. Revenues from fiscal reforms can be used to compensate low-income households, mitigate negative and increase positive social impacts of activities, reduce inequality, and promote inclusive growth (T10.4). Reforming fossil fuel subsidies (T12c) is another way to reduce inequalities, supporting SDG10, because these subsidies mainly benefit wealthy firms and consumers.

Goal 11: Sustainable city and communities. Fiscal policies (e.g. air pollution charges, landfill taxes, congestion charges, incineration taxes, vehicle taxes) can improve air quality and municipal and other waste management and reduce the adverse per capita environmental impacts of cities (T11.6).

Goal 12: Responsible consumption and production. Fiscal policies (e.g. air pollution charges, material taxes, taxes/fees on forestry and fisheries, waste taxes, product taxes) can motivate sustainable management and efficient use of natural resources (T12.2), reduce the release of chemicals (T12.4), and reduce food waste (T12.3) and waste generation (T12.5). In addition, tax reforms and the phaseout of harmful fossil fuel subsidies can reduce wasteful consumption (T12c) and increase the effectiveness of public spending.

Goal 13: Climate action. Revenues from fiscal instruments can support investments to strengthen resilience and adaptive capacities (T13.1), contribute to climate financing pledges (T13.a), and build capacities (T13.b). Fiscal incentives (e.g. vehicle taxes) can shift consumer behaviour towards low-carbon choices, accompanying efforts to improve education and raise awareness on climate change (T13.3).

Goal 14: Life below water. Fiscal policies (e.g. levies on marine aggregates, charges on ship emissions, plastic bag taxes) can help prevent and reduce marine pollution (T14.1) and support sustainable management and protection of marine and coastal ecosystems (T14.2). In addition, the elimination of fisheries subsidies (T14.6) will support SDG14.

Goal 17: Partnership for growth. Fiscal policies strengthen domestic resource mobilization (T17.1) and can help mobilize other sources of financing, including from the private sector (T17.3). Fiscal restructuring or reform optimizes state revenues, controls budget deficits and reduces debt-to-GDP ratios, and can contribute to long-term debt sustainability (T17.4.) Fiscal incentives for clean technologies can stimulate the development, transfer, dissemination and diffusion of environmentally sound technologies (T17.7).

We must, however, keep in mind that governments spend money on defence and security. On average, 40% of African states have some type of conflict at any point in time, and spending for weapons and war has its own economy.[172] Violent conflict necessarily results in destruction, such as happened in Libya during the downfall of Gadhafi. The cycle of development has to rebegin. Schumpeter[173] argues that a fiscal crisis pushes a state forward yet considers the destruction a crisis can cause; a country may have good leadership through a crisis where there is violence and destruction and loss of human and financial resources, but it may simultaneously have poor social welfare services and infrastructure.

And let us not forget that a government, like a human being, often spends more or less than anticipated. When this happens, there must be a commensurate adjustment to the national budget and often to tax rates. Progressive tax systems have the potential to reduce or

---

[172] Armed conflict location and event data project (2014)
[173] Schumpeter (1942)

tackle inequality, but they must be linked to effective expenditure of tax revenue and responsive welfare/benefit systems to realize sustainable development. However, if some poor people pay more in taxes than they receive in transfers, the objectives of a progressive system may be compromised. It is argued however that "making the system as a whole progressive does not require every individual tax to be progressive."[174] Emphasizing that higher income earners should provide a larger portion of domestic resource mobilisation helps ensure that tax burdens are distributed equitably.

2.3. Conclusion

No sun sets without its histories.

Zulu proverb

Fiscal legitimacy is a goal every state should seek no matter what the size of the budget, and this can only be achieved by ensuring that the fiscal system is accountable, responsible, transparent, efficient, effective, fair, and just. However, these principles need to be applied across the governance system of the state, to the financial theory of the state, its form of government and administration, how it finances the state and its public enterprises, and the interactions between the state and all stakeholders, including most importantly society.

African countries straddle the categorizations[175] as tribute, domain, tax and fiscal states. Other principles and philosophies must also be reflected upon to clarify the direction in which law and society interact to allow rulers to codify fiscal laws to enable the collection and redistribution of domestic resources. Fiscal legitimacy should be at the core of domestic resource mobilisation by the state. In addition, principles of legitimacy should be deepened through all levels of government and constituent stakeholders. Those involved include people who reflect upon fiscal law and taxation, because the theoretical building blocks are important in understanding and guiding, and those who make, apply, and abide by fiscal law.

---

[174] Mirrlees et al. (2011) p. 26
[175] Ormrod, Bonney and Bonney (1999)

Chapter 3

Systems of Fiscal Law and Policy

Wealth, if you use it, comes to an end;
learning, if you use it, increases.

Swahili proverb

Chapter 1 set out the African context: its economies, fiscal history, and current fiscal systems as well as diverse challenges facing fiscal collection and redistribution in specific countries. Chapter 2 brought forward the concepts of fiscal principles and fiscal legitimacy, as lenses through which to understand fiscal law, taxation, and the financing of African development. It also identified key parts of fiscal revenues and expenditures. It argued that the principles of accountability, responsibility, transparency, efficiency, and effectiveness are all held within a basket woven of fairness and justice.

This chapter delves into types of fiscal systems in place, in theory and in reality, in different African states. Understanding the systems in place informs the process of selecting appropriate systems for particular state contexts. Wealth, if used, will end, but learning about wealth and managing wealth are pathways to increasing it. This chapter discusses learnings from different types of fiscal systems in Africa. We discuss centralised and decentralised models, movement from a dominant revenue source to a system of multiple taxes, tax administration, and the productivity of various taxes.

3.1. Centralised and decentralised models

If your cornfield is far from your house,
the birds will eat your corn.

Congolese proverb

The African Charter for Popular Participation in Development and Transformation characterizes Africa as overcentralised and calls for participation of the people in the development of policies, programmes, and processes.[176] This is fundamental to the way forward. Several African countries have implemented forms of decentralised government, to facilitate the participation of people in government, i.e. Ethiopia, Nigeria, South Africa and Kenya, but this does not make the countries fiscally decentralised.

There are three main possibilities for the administration of fiscal systems: (1) a system where responsibilities and financing are managed in one place, usually in a centralised government with a unitary system, (2) a system where responsibilities and financing are delegated to administrative units closer to the people, and (3) a system that is a mixture, with some functions and finance undertaken at central level and others devolved or delegated to lower administrative levels.[177]

The question that comes to mind is: Which systems are best suited for African states and regions and even the continent? The answer is not simple or easy. This chapter will not attempt to answer the question, but it will describe the diverse options and how they are being used on the African continent, to inspire continued debate and discussion. Until the suboptimal compromise is reached, there are three choices: the centralised system, the decentralised system, or the mixed system which is a combination of the two.

3.1.1. Unitary or centralised system

Most countries in Africa are unitary systems. A unitary government need not have its taxing and spending powers specified in the constitution, but a federation by necessity must have them so specified. Fiscal arrangements related to taxing and spending powers are at the core of the contract between the constituent governments which combine to form the federation, as is the case of Nigeria and South Africa. Even though the central government necessarily must have fiscal powers, the composing units retain a sovereign right to conduct fiscal transactions of their own. The fiscal powers of a

---

[176] UNECA (1990)
[177] Ahmad, Devarajan, Khemani and Shah (2005)

central government are often laid out in constitutional provisions, which could be further defined by judicial interpretations.[178]

Commonly centralised functions include: (1) taxing powers and expenditure functions, (2) a uniformity rule stating that all taxes shall be uniform throughout the country, (3) an apportionment rule making the way for uniform and nationwide income tax, and (4) the prohibition of export taxes. Certain limitations could also be set out, for example: constituted decentralised administrative units like states, districts, or counties are prohibited from imposing taxes not only on exports but also on imports. An immunity provision forbids centralised taxation of states or counties and also applies in reverse.

3.1.2. Devolved or decentralised system

Devolution or decentralisation involves the transfer of political, administrative and fiscal management rights, duties and powers between the central or national government and lower levels of government. Such transfer of authority also includes the transfer of responsibility and accountability from the central or national government to the semi-autonomous subnational units. The theoretical argument for the transfer of responsibilities to lower levels of government is that the closer proximity of local policymakers or leaders to citizens increases the flow of information and better enables members of the public to understand, monitor and hold to account government officers.[179] As a result, the elected leaders in the devolved units tend to focus on improving service delivery so as to get re-elected. Devolved governance, it is argued, encourages greater citizen vigilance.[180] As regards fiscal decentralisation, it is important to note that the power to charge taxes generally involves three elements: tax structure design, tax administration, and tax revenue reporting and auditing.

According to Kiser and Sacks, the evaluation of devolution in African states shows mixed results. In theory, decentralisation "puts administration closer to the people, increasing their ability to control

---

[178] Kipngetich (2001) p. 4
[179] Hasnain (2008); Heald and McLeod (2010); Brosio and Outreville (2011) pp. 7-14
[180] Wagana, Iravo, Nzulwa and Kihoro (2016) p. 306

it."[181] While devolution may increase administrative efficiency and legitimise local governments over the national government, decentralisation of tax administration is not perfect. One of the negative effects of decentralisation, according to Kiser and Sacks, is the increasing number of legal instruments at the local government level as has happened in Uganda, Zimbabwe and Kenya.

Constitutional provisions regarding fiscality and taxation are multiple. Several state constitutions contain tax and expenditure limits. Some of these limitations are of a substantive character, in that they limit the amount of debt that can be incurred, the rate of taxation, or the growth in the rate of spending. Other limitations are of a procedural character, in that they provide that certain forms of debt must be approved in a popular vote, or they require a supermajority vote before legislatures can levy taxes or incur debts. And then there are assorted other public finance provisions, including requirements that taxes and appropriations be dedicated to a public purpose, as well as requirements that legislatures adopt a balanced budget. It was pointed out that over the last few years, legislatures have developed all sorts of creative ways to circumvent these constitutional limitations, in part through the redefinition of taxes, debts, and public entities so that they are not subject to these constitutional provisions.

Regarding fiscal management powers, fiscal decentralisation can, generally, take three forms, namely: full fiscal autonomy, assigned revenues system, and fiscal transfers and equalisation system.[182]

3.1.2.1. *Fiscal autonomy*

Under a full fiscal autonomy arrangement, the devolved units are solely dependent on their own resources. This means that both expenditure functions and revenue raising functions have been devolved to the subnational units. The devolved units, therefore, have the power not only to levy taxes but also to legislate on fiscal policies determining their tax bases, capacity among other things. Advocates of this arrangement argue that if each devolved unit

---

[181] Kiser and Sacks (2009) p. 192

[182] Ahmad, Devarajan, Khemani and Shah (2005)

depends solely upon its own taxable resources, there will be an incentive to lower tax rates in order to attract more economic activity and thus taxable capacity. Further, they affirm that politicians ought to, generally, be responsible for raising most of the money they spend.[183]

3.1.2.2. *Assigned revenues system*

Under an assigned revenues system, each devolved unit receives taxation revenue generated within its jurisdiction. It is important to note that this could apply to all taxes, with the total(s) forming the budget constraint of the devolved unit, or in the alternative to certain taxes only. In the latter scenario, the result would be that assigned revenues would constitute one element of a portfolio of revenue sources for the devolved units. In both scenarios, however, the devolved units have the mandate to levy the affected taxes in totality (i.e. the units have the power to charge the taxes and to legislate on all taxation policy issues incidental thereto).

3.1.2.3. *Fiscal transfers*

In a system of fiscal transfers, the central government usually retains principal control of tax revenues, although the devolved units are constitutionally mandated to levy certain categories of taxes. Fiscal decentralisation in this form is characterized by dependency of the devolved units on transfers from the central government and is largely expenditure based as opposed to revenue based. According to most taxation experts, devolution usually presents challenges with respect to tax revenue collection or administration.

Under the fiscal transfers and equalisation system, the resources and needs of each devolved unit are taken into consideration in the determination and allocation of transfers to the devolved units. This is usually because all the devolved jurisdictions differ in terms of taxable capacity, population density and developmental or infrastructure needs per capita.

---

[183] Heald and McLeod (2010) p. 4

3.2. From dominant revenue source to system of multiple taxes

There are several instances of a fiscal system relying on a dominant source of revenue. Nigeria until 2018 relied on oil rent for over 50% of its revenue.[184] In other cases, the system may be reliant on government business in agriculture or the extractives sector. Some counties may rely predominantly on aid. In the 1990s and early 2000s, many African countries relied almost completely on budget aid and debt to support their national budgets.[185] Today, each system faces its challenges, but most African countries rely at least in part on taxes and less on natural resources which are quickly being depleted.[186] The number of taxes implemented and the levels of government at which tax can be levied vary. Though varied, the systems come in three main forms: no taxes, single tax, and multiple taxes.

Of late, several independent states in conflict or emerging from conflict, like South Sudan, Somalia and Libya, and sometimes with huge amounts of natural resources, did not or could not collect any taxes. Other countries may simply have one tax operating in a state, for example, the Gulf states began in 2017 implementing only a VAT as a single tax, however, this is a rare occurrence in today's financially constrained world.[187] This implementation of one tax is considered more certain, more equitable, and cost effective.[188] It is also useful in post-conflict states, young/new states, and societies that did not previously have any taxes in order to gently introduce their populations to paying taxes.

Historical examples of a single tax in a simple form is the poll tax or head tax. It imposes tax on a person simply because the person exists in society, and it does not rely on income or trade. In countries such as Kenya,[189] Uganda, South Africa, Zimbabwe, and Sierra Leone, historically this took the form of the hut tax. It has been argued that poll tax is almost neutral and does not distort the pattern

---

[184] Odhiambo, O. and Olushola (2018)
[185] Omotola and Sailu (2009) p. 87
[186] OECD (2016a) chapter 1
[187] Zubeldia (2017)
[188] For example, the Islamic system of taxation follows this principle.
[189] Waris (2013a)

of economic activity. It has also been argued that it could be adjusted easily to the needs of the government and that every member of a society contributed to the upkeep of government, making the tax widespread while instilling a sense of awareness and responsibility in the minds of the taxpayer regarding the activities of the government.

The poll tax, however, does not address the wealth and income inequalities within a country, hurts poorer sections of the country more than the richer sections, and will hold the poor sections to change their consumption patterns while having no effect on the richer sections. In addition, the poll tax is not likely to provide sufficient tax revenue, and it would have to be fixed with reference to the poorest of the country.[190] The use of poll tax was there in ancient Greece, Rome, Britain, and even some colonies.[191] In post-genocide Rwanda, the Kagame government debated the possibility of implementing a flat tax.[192]

A single tax has many limitations. Can it distinguish between economic and business rent? Why should economic rent attract the levy while other forms of capital gains remain exempt? The levy would never provide adequate revenue nor assist in economic growth or other societal objectives. The movement to a multiple tax system becomes inevitable. It would be highly unjust to tax selectively, and a mixture of taxes is considered best to minimise the possible ill effects of the overreliance on one type of tax and to strengthen the beneficial effects of each in order to create a balanced and fair system.

3.3. Tax administration

The choice of a tax administration system is usually influenced by operational costs and efficiency rates, among other considerations.[193] There are four broad categories of institutional

---

[190] Bhatia (2018)

[191] In the history of taxation in Kenya, the first form of tax introduced during colonialism was the poll or hut tax, as it was known, where taxation was levied by the colonial government on each hut that was owned by a person. The purpose of this tax was to reduce polygamy and at the same time introduce the people to a monetary economy that would in turn support the activities of the colonial government.

[192] UNCTAD (2012) pp. 7 and 17

[193] OECD (2008)

arrangements with regard to tax revenue collection, including in economies with a dominant revenue source (see next section) and in economies trying to diversify. These are: single directorate in ministry of finance; multiple directorates in ministry of finance; unified semi-autonomous body; and unified semi-autonomous body with board.[194]

Under the first arrangement of a single directorate in the ministry of finance, tax administration functions are the responsibility of a single organizational unit located within the structure of the Ministry of Finance or its equivalent. Under the multiple directorates arrangement, tax administration and collection functions are the responsibility of multiple organizational units located within the Ministry of Finance. It is important to note that these units usually comprise the respective revenue bodies for the subnational regions or units. Under the third arrangement of a unified semi-autonomous body, tax administration functions are the responsibility of the semi-autonomous revenue body, the head of which reports to a government minister. Finally, under the fourth arrangement, tax administration functions are the responsibility of a unified semi-autonomous body, the head of which reports to a minister and a board of management consisting of external officials.

The performance indicators of such tax administration units or revenue bodies generally revolve around:[195]

i)   taxpayer satisfaction with services delivered and overall perceptions of agency management of the tax system;
ii) rates of taxpayers' compliance achieved;
iii) compliance burden reduction; and
iv) perception of employee engagement or satisfaction.

The Tanzanian Revenue Authority (TRA), for example, employs about 3,600 people, which is a lot compared to only 1,500 in Uganda and 250 in Rwanda. However, if you look at the global average of 0.82 tax staff for every 1,000 citizens, the TRA is not doing well with 0.087 per 1,000 citizens.[196] In theory, the personnel are well trained, but a recent case about forged degrees shows that many unqualified

---

[194] OECD (2008) p. 12
[195] OECD (2008) p. 58
[196] Chr. Michelsen Institute (CMI, 2011) in OECD (2014) p. 13

people hold offices. In April 2017, almost 10,000 civil servants were fired because of this. Furthermore, there is no university program on taxation, and therefore the TRA probably lacks well-trained staff, which is not an exception among national revenue authority staff.[197]

Governments impose many types of taxes. While taxpayers may assess, compute and pay taxes, revenue authorities are also empowered by the law to demand taxes. For example, the Kenya Revenue Authority Act empowers the Kenya Revenue Authority to collect and receive all the revenue on behalf of the Government of Kenya.[198] In most countries, individuals pay income taxes when they earn money, consumption taxes when they spend it, property taxes when they own a home or land, and in some cases estate taxes when they die.

In Nigeria, the Federal Inland Revenue Service is empowered under Section 8 of the Nigerian Federal Inland Revenue Service (Establishment) Act[199] to assess, collect, account and enforce payment of taxes as may be due to the Government or any of its agencies. In Morocco, it is the General Tax Administration that performs these functions at both the state and local levels.[200] In most African countries, both the national and local governments (in devolved systems) similarly collect tax. In Guinea in 1990,[201] taxes were predominantly levied for the benefit of the federal state; only a minimum tax for local development and a tax on firearms was levied by local authorities. The revenue of the local administration was insufficient.[202] The National Directorate of Taxes is comprised of 33 fiscal administration prefectures, seven administrative regions, plus the city of Conakry which enjoys a particular status of decentralised community.[203]

---

[197] Ng'wanakilala (2017)
[198] Republic of Kenya (1995) section 5(1)
[199] Republic of Nigeria (2007)
[200] Kingdom of Morocco (2019)
[201] Republic of Guinea (1990) articles 339-354
[202] Note that Code was updated January 2019: www.lgdj.fr/guinee-code-general-des-impots-2019-9782353081837.html
[203] Republic of Guinea (2018)

3.4. Productivity of various taxes

No one gets a mouthful of food by
picking between another person's teeth.

Igbo proverb

Generally, a tax must have the approval of society, through the constitution or legislature, or other participatory decision-making processes involving public debates and pressure groups, for example. We generally assume that the government has an efficient and transparent administrative mission through which the tax system can be enforced. However, the theory and practice of tax structure and policy can be at variance with each other, and quite often a tax proposal, which theoretically may be quite sound and desirable, would have to be left out from a practical point of the view.

The government's job in this sector is to predetermine the productivity of a tax for it to be justified. If a tax is unlikely to be productive, it is advisable to avoid it. The productivity of a tax is measured by the revenue yield versus the cost of administering it or efficiency cost and the estimated revenues versus the actual revenue.

Tax revenue is divided into three sections. First, *taxes on income and expenditure*. This includes taxes, levied on the receipts of income and expenditure, such as corporation tax, expenditure tax, interested tax, and any other similar taxes. Second, *tax on property and capital transactions*. This includes taxes on specific forms of wealth and its transfers such as estate duty, wealth tax, gift tax, house tax, land revenue and stamp duty[204], and registration fees. Third, *tax on commodities and services*. This includes taxes on the production, sale, purchase, transport, storage, and consumption of goods and services.

Taxes themselves are classified into three main categories, according to the *impact and incidence* of tax, the *object that is subject* to the tax, and the *tax rate* that is applicable. Impact of tax means the persons on whom the tax is imposed, and the incidence of tax refers

---

[204] "Stamp duty is tax levied on various transactions such as transfer of properties, shares and stocks. [In Kenya, it] is collected by the Ministry of Lands, which has seconded the function to Kenya Revenue Authority (KRA). [...] Stamp duty is major revenue earner for the Government." Odhiambo, F. T. (2011)

to the person who must bear the burden of the tax.[205] Under this classification there are two types of taxes: Direct Tax and Indirect Tax.

3.3.1. Direct tax

Both the impact and incidence of a direct tax is on the same person. The tax requires that a taxpayer remit their taxes to the tax authority directly. Dalton describes a direct tax as one which is "really paid by the person on whom it is legally imposed."[206] In other words, a direct tax as one which is demanded from the person for whom it was intended. Examples of direct taxes include income tax, death duty, corporation tax, wealth tax, expenditure tax, withholding tax, and advance tax.

There are several advantages of direct taxes. First, they are based on the canon of equity and as such the burden is equitably distributed. Due to its progressive nature, as the income of a person increases, the rate of income tax also increases. Second, direct taxes are also based on the canon of certainty as to the time, amount and way the tax is expected to be paid. The government is also in a better position to plan, because it is certain as to the amount it expects to receive from the taxpayers. Third, the cost of collection is low, and thus this type of tax satisfies the canon of economy. The taxpayer makes the payment directly to the government. Fourth, direct tax satisfies the canon of elasticity due to its flexibility. The government can easily increase or decrease the rate of taxation as it deems necessary. Fifth, direct taxes are easily understood by the taxpayer. Sixth, direct taxes are based on the canon of desirability and thus are only paid by those who are subject to it. For instance, only employed persons are subject to income tax.

Seventh, direct taxes are useful for the purpose of wealth redistribution and reduction of income and wealth inequalities. The progressive nature of direct tax ensures that the poor whose incomes are below the minimum tax limit are exempt from income tax. On the other hand, those who earn high salaries pay a commensurate

---

[205] Waris (2013a) p. 19
[206] Dalton (2009), p. 33

higher amount of tax. In this manner, the direct taxes fulfil the need of the central authority for social and economic justice and fairly reflect changes in people's incomes.

Finally, direct tax promotes a spirit of civic responsibility among taxpayers. Taxpayers are conscious that they are paying taxes to the government, therefore they take an interest in the activities of the government, putting a check on the misuse of public funds. The government is in turn obliged to incur public expenditure for public welfare purposes.

Disadvantages of direct taxes are several. First, direct taxes are unpopular because the taxpayer must pay them directly out of their incomes. Second, direct taxes violate the principle of convenience, because they are often paid in a lump sum. Furthermore traders, businesspeople, and producers among others are forced to comply with formalities relating to their income. The requirements are complicated, and thus income tax experts become necessary to assist such self-employed persons to fully comply with the stipulations of the law. Third, direct taxes are levied at the discretion of the government, which fixes the rates and interprets the tax. This lack of inclusion of other parties harbours an element of arbitrariness. Fourth, direct taxes are an inconvenience, and thus taxpayers will try to evade paying them and sometimes even consult tax experts on how to avoid taxes. This cultivates a culture of dishonesty and can lead to loss of revenue for the government.

Fifth, direct taxes are not imposed on all income groups; low-income earners do not contribute anything to the exchequer through direct taxation. Sixth, direct taxes adversely affect savings and investment because the higher the income level, the higher the tax rate, thus denying that taxpayer the opportunity to save or invest more. This in turn discourages people from working more. Finally, corporate tax serves to discourage industries and firms which are engaged in the production of essential goods.

All African countries levy an income tax, however, with some variations. In some countries, like Rwanda, all earnings are taxable, no matter how low.[207] Other countries have a minimum below which

---

[207] Republic of Rwanda (2005)

persons are not taxed. For example, in Namibia, below an annual salary of 50,000 Namibian dollars (approx. 3,500 USD), persons are not taxed,[208] and in Kenya the first 125 USD is tax exempt for income tax.[209] In both countries, those not taxed include house help and nannies as well as construction labourers and some nursery and early primary school teachers.

For corporations the income tax rates vary between 3% and 15% in Mauritius, 28% in South Africa and 30% in Kenya. This inequality in how corporate taxpayers are treated, by subjecting them to different rates of taxation within and across countries, breaches the canon of equity and creates tax competition. In addition, the different rates based on the amount an individual earns versus a corporation lead to a contravention of Ibn Khaldun's principle of justice and fairness.[210]

3.3.1.1. *Personal income tax*

An individual income tax, also called a personal income tax (PIT), is a tax on a person's income. Income includes wages, salaries, and other earnings from one's occupation; interest earned by savings accounts and certain types of bonds; rents (earnings from rented properties); royalties earned on sales of patented or copyrighted items, such as inventions and books; and dividends from stock. Income also includes capital gains, which are profits from the sale of stock, real estate, or other investments whose value has increased over time. The Republic of Guinea was ranked 182nd of 190 economies on the ease of paying taxes.[211] In the ongoing process of decentralisation, a Local Government Code[212] was adopted in 2006. This Code called for autonomy in creating and collecting taxes and setting tax rates for local governments.

The national government of many African countries requires citizens to file an individual income tax return each year. In countries like Uganda, Nigeria and Kenya, computation of tax liability and

---

[208] PricewaterhouseCoopers (2018)
[209] Republic of Kenya (2012)
[210] Khaldun (1377)
[211] World Bank (2018) p. 164
[212] Republic of Guinea (2006)

filing of tax returns is fully automated through an electronic tax platform. Each taxpayer must compute their tax liability – the amount of money they owe the government. This computation involves four major steps. First, the taxpayer computes adjusted gross income – one's income from all taxable sources minus certain expenses incurred in earning that income.

Second, the taxpayer converts adjusted gross income to taxable income – the amount of income subject to tax – by subtracting various amounts called exemptions and deductions. Some deductions exist to enhance the fairness of the tax system. Other deductions are meant to encourage certain kinds of behaviour. For example, some governments permit deductions of charitable contributions as an incentive for individuals to give money to worthy causes.

Third, the taxpayer calculates the amount of tax due by consulting a tax table, which shows the exact amount of tax due for most levels of taxable income. People with very high incomes consult a rate schedule, a list of tax rates for different ranges of taxable income, to compute the amount of tax due.

Finally, the taxpayer subtracts taxes paid during the year and any allowable tax credits to arrive at the final tax liability. After computing the amount of tax due, the taxpayer must send this information to the government and enclose the amount due. Many taxpayers, rather than owing money, receive a refund from the government after filing a tax return, typically because they had too much tax withheld from their wages and salaries during the year.

Income taxation enjoys widespread support, because income is considered a good indicator of an individual's ability to pay. However, income taxes are hard to administer because measuring income is often difficult. For example, some people receive part of their income "in-kind" – in the form of goods and services rather than in cash. Farmers provide field hands with food, and corporations may give employees access to company cars and free parking spaces. If governments tax cash income but not in-kind compensation, then people can avoid taxation by taking a higher proportion of their income as in-kind compensation.

Whereas an income tax is levied on all sources of income, a payroll tax applies only to wages and salaries. Employers automatically withhold payroll taxes from employees' wages and forward them to the government. Payroll taxes are the main sources of funding for various social insurance programs, such as those that provide benefits to the poor, elderly, unemployed, and disabled. Although the legislators who set up payroll taxes intended to divide the tax burden equally between employers and employees, this may not occur in practice. Some economists believe that the tax causes employers to offer lower pre-tax wages to employees than they would otherwise, in effect shifting the tax burden entirely to employees.

3.3.1.2. Corporate income tax

Corporations in most, if not all, African countries, resident or non-resident, must pay tax on their net income (profits) to the government. In Kenya, for example, there is a single flat rate for all companies, while in other countries the rate may differ. In Morocco, for instance, the rate is progressive, and ranges between 10% and 30% on corporate income exceeding 1 million Moroccan dirhams. Additionally, a higher rate of 37% is applied to leasing and credit companies. In Nigeria, the rate is 30% for both resident and non-resident companies, and in South Africa, a flat rate of 28% is imposed.

The corporate income tax (CIT) is one of the most controversial types of taxes. Although the law treats corporations as if they have an independent ability to pay a tax, many economists note that only real people – such as the shareholders who own corporations – can bear a tax burden. In addition, the CIT leads to double taxation of corporate income. Income is taxed once when the corporation declares its profits and a second time when the taxed profits are paid out to shareholders in the form of dividends, which dividends are also taxed. Thus, corporate income faces a higher tax burden than income earned by individuals or by other types of businesses.

African countries may deal with this issue by lowering the tax rate for dividends. In the case of Kenya, dividends from a company are not usually subject to additional tax except withholding tax, and if the company is listed on the stock exchange then there is a possibility of capital gains taxes, but since 2016 shares in the stock exchange are exempt. It is also important to note that under the current tax regime, dividends from foreign companies are not taxable. In Morocco, dividends of resident companies are usually included in their business profits but are 100% deductible for purposes of calculating taxable income.

Some economists have proposed abolishing the CIT and instead taxing the owners of corporations (shareholders) through the PIT. Other students of the tax system see the CIT as the price corporations pay in return for special privileges from society at a reduced rate. The most important of these privileges is limited liability for shareholders. This means that creditors cannot claim the personal assets of shareholders, because the liability of shareholders for the corporation's debts is limited to the amount they have invested in the corporation.

In some jurisdictions, companies are also subject to capital gains taxes with respect to gains made from the transfer of qualifying property and assets, which could include money, land, choses in action[213], and other immovable property. Countries such as South Africa, Rwanda, Tanzania and Kenya have imposed a capital gains tax on companies. In Kenya, however, as of 1 January 2016, companies are exempted from capital gains with respect to shares traded in the securities exchange and that are licensed by the Capital Markets Authority. In certain countries, capital gains tax may be excluded in instances where the country has a double taxation agreement (DTA) with another country. For example, in Rwanda, capital gains tax is exempted for companies of countries with which Rwanda has a DTA in place, including South Africa, Belgium and Mauritius.

3.3.2. Indirect tax

An indirect tax is that tax under which the impact of the tax is on one person while the incidence is on another person. Indirect tax is

---

[213] A chose in action consists of the "bundle of personal rights over property which can only be claimed or enforced by action, and not by taking physical possession, for example, a cash balance at a bank or money due on a bond." https://uk.practicallaw.thomsonreuters.com

commonly defined as a tax demanded from one person in the expectation and intention that he shall indemnify himself at the expense of another. Thus, the tax operates on the principle of shifting the tax burden from the seller to the buyer. This is classification according to method of collection. An indirect tax is one collected directly from the source, the taxpayer, that the law intended but is not necessarily the person who submits the money to the revenue collection agency. It is been claimed that taxes on income are direct, while those on consumption are indirect.

In the case of indirect tax, the intended taxpayer passes over the payment or tax burden to another person who ends up paying the tax. Indirect taxes may be specific or *ad valorem* (added value). When they are imposed per item or on a per unit basis, they are called specific. On the other hand, when the tax amount is scheduled according to the value of the item being taxed, it is *ad valorem*. Sales tax is mostly *ad valorem*. Excise duties are sometimes specific and sometimes *ad valorem* and sometimes a combination of both. The advantage of *ad valorem* taxes is that the tax is automatically hinged on to the value of the item and moves along with it. Thus, tax incidence is split into two: legal incidence where the tax burden is legally imposed and economic incidence, which is the actual monetary burden. These taxes include VAT, custom duty and sales tax.

There are several advantages of indirect taxes. First, indirect taxes are convenient, because they are paid in small amounts when a good or a service is purchased. They are less burdensome than direct taxes, because buyers feel less the pinch of the tax, which is included in the prices of commodities. Second, indirect taxes are amenable to a change in government. A new government can reduce or increase the rates of the tax payable, which makes the indirect tax flexible or elastic in nature. Third, indirect taxes are an economic tax; producers and sellers have the responsibility to collect and remit the tax directly to the government. Fourth, indirect taxes are included in the prices of goods and services purchased, so there are fewer possibilities for evasion of the taxes. Wholesalers and retailers simply play the role of collector, and thus they are not pained when remitting the tax to the government. A customer can usually avoid paying this tax only by avoiding the purchase of goods and services. Producers, wholesalers, and retailers evade this type of tax by selling products which are not entered into their stocklist and by not issuing a receipt for the sale of goods.

Fifth, indirect taxes can be useful in restricting consumption of harmful goods, for example goods that pose a danger to the consumer's health. The government levies heavy taxes on items like cigarettes and alcohol, causing their prices to increase so as to reduce their consumption. Finally, indirect taxes are a tool the government uses to implement economic policies. Indirect taxes can be levied on imported goods thereby making them more expensive and thus less competitive, giving room to locally produced goods which will be more competitive due to their low prices. The government may also encourage the development of an industry by lowering or eliminating indirect taxes levied on it.

There are several disadvantages of indirect taxes. First, indirect taxes are not a certain source of revenue, because the government cannot determine sales. If a good is not necessary to consumers, an upward price change may negatively impact its demand and consequently the revenue collected. Second, an indirect tax is a regressive tax in nature which means that, irrespective of the purchasing power of the consumer, all buyers pay the same tax rate. It therefore fails to fulfil the overarching principle of justice as espoused by Ibn Khaldun and the canon of equity, because the tax burden is heavier on the poor. Third, the indirect tax becomes expensive for the state, which must employ inspectors to check to ensure that producers, wholesalers and retailers are paying the taxes as required.

Fourth, the effect of an indirect tax is an increase in price, which has a direct impact on demand. When demand for a good or service falls due to a price increase, it directly affects production and consequently employment and job opportunity. Fifth, indirect taxes work to escalate inflation due to their effect on the prices of products. The higher costs of goods lead to a demand for higher wages, which triggers a further increase in prices. Finally, because indirect taxes are included in prices, taxpayers may be less conscious, than when paying direct taxes, that they are indeed paying taxes when they purchase goods and services. This lack of understanding may lead to the taxpayer not demanding from the tax authorities a proper account on how such monies are spent.

From the perspective of Ibn Khaldun and fiscal legitimacy, indirect taxes tend to be oppressive to the poor and give the wealthy preference in that all pay the same rates, based on their consumption. In addition, in developing countries facing challenges of food security, basic foods tend to attract VAT, and this can acerbate food insecurity. Indirect taxes ought to be avoided completely if a state is attempting to develop its fiscal legitimacy and the relationship between the state and society. There are also gender considerations. "Indirect taxes in Ghana [...] have a greater impact on women, as they spend a higher percentage of their income on consumer goods."[214] Note, from the same source, that:

> Women in developing countries tend to purchase more goods and services that promote health, education and nutrition compared to men. This creates the potential for women to bear a larger VAT burden if the VAT system does not provide for exemptions, reduced rates or zero-rating.

Additional questions going forward include possibly considering data as a commodity[215] and determining what in the digital economy to tax, or not, by whom and how[216]. There are also arguments that "any changes to tax rules should focus on wider developments in ways of doing business and on intangible investment rather than just digitalization."[217]

3.3.2.1. General sales tax

A general sales tax imposes the same tax rate on a wide variety of goods and, in some cases, services. Although sellers are legally responsible for paying sales taxes, and sellers collect sales taxes from consumers, the burden of any given sales tax is often divided between sellers and consumers. Most states exempt certain necessities from sales tax, such as basic groceries and prescription drugs. Both

---

[214] GTZ/GIZ (no date) p. 2
[215] Thornhill (2018)
[216] Wolfers (2018)
[217] Ho and Turley (2018)

individuals and businesses pay sales tax. In some African countries, Sales Taxes were replaced by the VAT.

3.3.2.2. Excise taxes

Federal/national, state/county, and municipal/local governments levy excise taxes, which are sales taxes on specific goods or services. Excise taxes are also called selective sales taxes. Goods subject to excise taxes in African countries include tobacco products, alcoholic beverages, gasoline, and some luxury items. Excise taxes are applied either on a per unit basis, such as per package of cigarettes or per litre or gallon of gasoline, or as a fixed percentage of the sales price.

Governments sometimes levy excise taxes to pay for specific projects. For example, voters in a city might approve a tax on hotel rooms to help pay for a new convention centre. Some national governments impose an excise tax on airline tickets to help pay for airport improvements or airline security. Revenues from gasoline taxes typically pay for highway construction and improvements. Excise taxes designed to limit consumption of a commodity, such as taxes on cigarettes and alcoholic beverages, are commonly known as "sin taxes."

Another type of excise tax is the license tax. Most states require people to buy licenses to engage in certain activities, such as hunting and fishing, operating a motor vehicle, owning a business, or selling alcoholic beverages. In most African countries, excise taxes are governed under an excise or customs duty act. In Morocco, it is the Customs and Excise Act, Cap 472 of 1994 (revised 2010[218]), in Nigeria it is the Customs and Excise Management Act. In Kenya, it is the Excise Duty Act, no. 23 of 2015.

3.3.2.3. Value-added tax

In most African countries, the favoured form of consumption taxation is a value-added tax (VAT), however, it was introduced by the IMF as part of their conditionalities and remains an unfair and regressive system. In this tax system, the seller pays the government

---

[218] See http://admin.theiguides.org/Media/Documents/customs-act-2010.pdf

a percentage of the value added to goods or services at each stage of production. The value added at each stage of production is the difference between the seller's costs for materials and the selling price. In essence, a VAT is just a general sales tax that is collected at multiple stages. The final consumer of the service or product pays VAT. In most African countries, the rate of VAT ranges anywhere between 0% and 20%. For example, in South Africa, the rate is 15%. The VAT rate in Nigeria is 5% with proposals to increase it to 15%. In Morocco, the standard rate is 20% with lower and varied rates for certain designated operations.

In East African countries, the VAT rate in the case of a zero-rated supply is 0% and in any other case is 18% of the taxable value of the taxable supply, the value of imported taxable goods, or the value of a supply of imported taxable services.[219] In the production of maize flour, for example, the farmer grows maize and sells it to a miller, who turns it into mealie flour. The miller sells the flour to a restaurant owner, who cooks and sells it, perhaps as corn bread or as ugali, to a consumer. At each stage, value is added to the commodity. The miller adds value by processing the corn with capital (machines) and labour. The farmer, the miller, and the restaurant owner each charge their customer a VAT. However, they can each claim a credit to recover the tax they paid on purchases related to their commercial activities, but the consumer cannot.

3.3.2.4. Tariffs

Tariffs, also called duties or customs duties, are taxes levied on imported or exported goods. Import duties are considered consumption taxes, because they are levied on goods to be consumed. Import duties also protect domestic industries from foreign competition by making imported goods more expensive than their domestic counterparts. With the coming into force of AfCFTA, the entire continent, it is expected, will be a customs-free zone.

---

[219] Republic of Kenya (2013) section 5

3.3.2.5. *Property taxes or capital gains tax*

In principle, a property tax is a tax on an individual's wealth – the value of all the person's assets, both financial (such as stocks and bonds) and real (such as houses, cars, and artwork). In practice, property taxes are usually more limited. In various African countries, governments generally levy property taxes on buildings – such as homes, office buildings, and factories – and on land. The property tax is by far the largest source of revenue for local governments.

The property tax is often unpopular with homeowners. One reason is that, because homes are not sold very often, governments must levy the tax on the estimated value of the dwelling. Some citizens believe that the government overvalues their homes, leading to unfairly high property tax burdens. Using Kenya as an example, a capital gains tax (CGT), was reintroduced on 1 January 2015 after being suspended in 1985. It is chargeable on the whole of a gain which accrues to a company or an individual on the transfer of property situated in Kenya. It applies to all transfers of property after 1 January 2015. CGT is paid by the seller at the rate of 5% and it is a final tax.[220]

This tax is unpopular for another reason as well. Huge amounts of land are held traditionally. If this land is ever sold, the tax would be calculated on the whole amount of the sale. Governments on the continent seem unaware of this dynamic and its impact. A similar challenge would face land transferred out of government illegally as a kickback, which is a form of corruption.

3.3.2.6. *Estate, inheritance and gift taxes*

When a person dies, the property they leave for others may be subject to tax. An estate tax is a tax on the deceased person's estate, which includes everything the person owned at the time of death – money, real estate, stock, bonds, proceeds from insurance policies, and material possessions. Most governments levy estate taxes before the deceased person's property passes to heirs, although many governments do not impose an estate tax on property inherited by a spouse. An inheritance tax also taxes the value of the deceased

---

[220] Republic of Kenya (2013) section 3(2)(f) and section 34

person's estate, but after the estate passes to heirs. The inheritors pay the tax. Estate and inheritance taxes are sometimes collectively called death taxes. A gift tax is a tax on the transfer of property between living people.

Estate and gift taxes are controversial. Proponents argue that they are useful tools for distributing wealth more equally in society and preventing the rise of powerful oligarchies. Opponents argue that it is a person's right to pass on property to his or her heirs, and the government has no right to interfere. If an individual has paid tax on his or her income while in the process of accumulating wealth, critics ask, why should it be taxed again when the wealth is transferred?

Others argue that estate and gift taxes discourage individuals from working and saving to accumulate wealth to leave to their children. On the other hand, the presence of an estate tax might encourage people to accumulate greater wealth in order to reach a given after-tax goal. There are no African countries currently charging their populations estate taxes.

3.3.3. Other taxes

A *poll tax*, also called a lump-sum tax or head tax, collects the same amount of money from each individual regardless of income or circumstances. Poll taxes are not widely used, because their burden falls hardest on the poor.

A *pollution tax* is a tax levied on a company that produces air, water, or soil pollution over a certain level established by the government. The tax provides an incentive for companies to pollute less and thus reduce damage to the environment. However, these taxes account for just a tiny amount of total tax revenue.

A *transaction tax* is a tax levied on financial transactions. This includes money transactions through banks, mobile phones or currency transactions.

3.5. Taxes based on tax base

The tax base is the object to which tax applies. For example, the tax base can include the following:

a. Current flows of income (where are subject to an income tax);
b. Property (subject to a property tax);
c. Sale price of goods sold (subject to as sales tax);
d. Value of goods exported (subject to an export tax);
e. Value of goods imported (subject to a customs/import tax); and
f. Stocks (subject to a capital gains tax).

A tax rate means the amount of tax per unit of a tax base. There are four ways to apply tax rates: progressive tax, proportional tax, regressive tax, and degressive tax.

3.5.1. Progressive tax

A tax is progressive when, with increasing income, the tax liability increases in absolute terms and in proportion to income. The progressive tax takes a larger proportion of people's income as their income increases. The tax liability increases both in absolute terms and in proportion to the increased income. Personal income tax is a good example of a progressive tax; it applies a graduated rate of tax, in relation to the income bracket of the person.

There are several advantages of a progressive tax. First, the progressive tax helps achieve the objective of wealth redistribution, because the wealthy pay more tax. Second, it is related to the ability to pay. Third, it is a productive tax, because as the earning power of society increases, so does the tax yield. Fourth, it brings about equality of sacrifice by ensuring that the more one earns the more tax one pays, and as such the level of sacrifice is maintained. Finally, it is economical to administer, because the cost of collection does not increase as the rate of tax goes up. The less tax the rich pay, the more likely they are used in income on luxuries increasing inequality. Second, in the absence of this tax it will lead to a concentration of economic power with the rich who may be tempted to misuse it. Third, this tax would endanger the productivity of the masses and can result in calls for social and political unrest. In addition, progressive taxes have a much lower cost of administration and collection.

Progressive tax also has disadvantages. First, where the tax rates are high, it will inhibit savings and investments. Second, the tax authorities do not engage taxpayers on the rates applicable, and the tax is thus arbitrary. Third, it is inconvenient on the taxpayer, because it must be paid in bulk. Finally, it operates on the assumption that all other factors affecting the taxpayer are the same, when the circumstances of each taxpayer differ from those of other taxpayers.

A very strong case for progressive taxes exists in terms of ability to pay and the corresponding sacrifice which taxation brings about. Lerner[221] argues that individual members of society who do not have the full capacity to join the tax base will still join and move towards income equality at a slow rate. Seligman however states that taxpayers will persist in activity which will check the progression of taxation that could bring about complete income equality. "Legal justice means legal equality; but a legal equality which would attempt to force an equality of fortune in the face of natural inequalities of ability would be a travesty of justice."[222] Wagner states that the tax system is a powerful instrument for correcting the distribution of income as determined by market forces and the institution of inheritance.[223]

3.5.2. Proportional tax

A tax is proportional if it increases in the same proportion to an increase in taxation. Proportional tax administration is simple. It is easily decided; enforcement and rates schedules are simple. However, in proportional tax would involve tax in the individual family in the society irrespective of the income levels.

The proportional tax sees the relative position of different taxpayers. All taxpayers use the same proportion of the purchasing power therefore proportion of tax is easy to understand. A proportional tax is one which charges the same rate or percentage irrespective of the level of income of the taxpayers. The advantages of the proportional tax are that it is a simple tax to administer and is neutral, because every taxpayer pays the same rate. However, the disadvantages of the proportional tax are that it is not an equitable tax because it is heavier on the poor, and it has a lower tax yield as compared to the progressive tax.

---

[221] Lerner (1959)
[222] Seligman (1908) p. 132
[223] Wagner (1880) pp. 381-85

3.5.3. Regressive tax

A regressive tax is one where tax liability falls with increase of income. A regressive tax is one which is heavier on the lower income earning taxpayers than on the rich. A proportional tax is a regressive tax. An example is the VAT, which is a fixed rate charged on goods and services, irrespective of the income earning power of the buyer. A regressive tax can be said to be the exact opposite of a progressive tax.

3.5.4. Degressive tax

A degressive tax is where income goes up, but tax liability goes down. A tax is said to be degressive if the high earning income taxpayers pay a relatively lower amount of tax. This occurs when a rate of progressive tax stops at some point, and the rate remains constant or is not as steep as it was previously. Income tax is an example of a degressive tax, once the rate of progression has reached the maximum rate; then from that point onwards, as the income levels continue to rise, the level of tax paid continues to reduce.

A degressive tax may also occur where a tax rate is set highest for a certain type or level of income which then bears the greatest burden of tax. From that point onwards, the tax is applied proportionately. On the other hand, as the income reduces, the rate also drops. An advantage of a degressive tax is that higher income earning taxpayers can save more and invest, and it motivates people to work harder to pay less tax when they earn more. A disadvantage of the degressive tax is that it is not practical.

3.6. Conclusion

Young birds will always open their mouths,
even to those who come to kill them.

Tswana proverb

Current fiscal systems begin with the setting of targets, and then the expenditure pots are juggled. It is a problem, however, when targets are set with no clear reference to spending, and the discomfort of a small tax base needs to be brought into focus. When the same tax base is repeatedly taxed from a myriad of different angles. Africans must not just watch fiscal law and policy systems unfold but proactively shape them, so they unfold in contextually appropriate and favourable ways. If not, the knowledge of the population will come of age, and people will realise which systems may be destroying their lives.

Chapter 4

Principles Guiding Budgeting of Revenue and Expenditure

The hyena with a cub does not consume all the available food.

Akamba proverb

The objective of revenue collection is to facilitate the realisation of certain goals. Revenue collection is guided by principles. Features of the fiscal structure should be devised in conformity with those principles. Objectives of the fiscal system in any economy relate to overall government policies. Objectives differ between and within countries. Objectives can be contradictory and could be partially resolved by the tax system.

A fiscal system cannot be expected to fully achieve all its intended goals. For example, VAT is considered an ideal form of indirect taxation, but its adoption in developing countries is not as it was designed. Suggestions for reforming direct taxation are many and include: replacing all direct taxes (or at least income tax) with the tax of expenditure,[224] or replacing direct personal taxes with a tax on personal consumption expenditure; consolidating all direct taxes into one tax; and coordinating all direct taxes such that they can be assessed simultaneously on the basis of a single comprehensive return.

Various committees and commissions have studied the problem of taxation and recommended its restructuring. For instance, after the 1954 report of the Income Tax Committee in Kenya and the 1956-57 report of the East African Commission of Inquiry on Income Tax, several other bodies were set up to study taxation.[225] After the 1970s, however, the same importance was unfortunately not given to taxation as was given, through various commissions, to other issues such as land and the constitution.[226]

Developing countries face the problems of insufficient savings and insufficient capital accumulation. There is a need to promote

[224] Prest (1979)
[225] See Gichuki (2015)
[226] Waris (2007) p. 289

specific products with good gaps between supply and demand. Finance for social welfare must be created and maintained. Basic industries must be developed to provide a foundation for the industrialisation of the economy. The removal of regional disparities necessitates the promotion of agricultural and industrial development in underdeveloped areas of countries and regions of the continent. Unnecessary imports should be restricted, and exports and import substitution should be encouraged.

An equitable and progressive tax system is likely to be a disincentive for savings and capital accumulation. A system of capital gains discourages building up of specific capital assets. Thus, a country like Kenya suffers from the characteristics of what is called a dual economy.[227] Traditionally, indirect taxation was advocated for developing countries as good for revenue collection and influencing resource allocation. It was argued that a country with inflationary tendencies should reduce the aggressiveness of taxation of capital goods, raw materials, and other intermediate goods. Commodity taxation should concentrate rather on final consumption goods only; the rates should be appropriate and the coverage highly selective. Luxuries and articles of conspicuous consumption should be taxed heavily, and necessities should be taxed at very low rates.

4.1. Budgetary systems

If you watch your pot,
your food will not burn.

Proverb from Mauritania, Nigeria, and Niger

The word "budget" comes from the old French word *bougette*, which means little bag. Initially, "budget" referred solely to the Chancellor's annual speech on the nation's finances. Later, the word became associated with a financial statement or plan in any context. Income taxes must be reaffirmed each year within a window of time in the budgeting process. If this deadline for agreement to pass the law is not met, the Government would lose its power to levy the tax

---

[227] Steele (1975)

and would have to repay the income tax collected. By convention, the Budget Speech is not interrupted. But this convention has become more honoured in breach than observance.

Even when fiscal resources are important, the issue of how governments decide what and how much to collect and spend is important. Thus, in recent years, interest has been increasing, both within and outside government, in how tax policy decisions are made and in who can influence policy outcomes.

4.1.1. Budgetary and fiscal policy

A single bracelet does not jingle.

Congolese proverb

Budgetary policy is policy in which the government sets out how it will collect and spend state resources to achieve certain goals. Macroeconomic policy is the tool used by government to control economic growth. Fiscal policy is the use of government spending to influence the economy.[228] Governments typically use fiscal policy to promote strong and sustainable growth and reduce poverty.[229] When policymakers seek to influence the economy, they have two main tools at their disposal: monetary policy and fiscal policy.

Central banks affect economic activities by influencing the money supply through adjustments to interest rates, bank reserves, and the purchase and sale of government securities and foreign exchange.[230] Governments influence the economy by changing the levels and types of taxes, the extent and composition of spending, and the degree and form of borrowing.

Governments directly and indirectly influence the ways resources are used in the economy. A basic equation of national income accounting that measures the output of an economy or gross domestic product (GDP) – according to expenditures – helps show how this happens. Fiscal policy that increases aggregate demand

---

[228] Easterly and Rebelo (1993)
[229] Horton and El-Ganainy (2018)
[230] Bajpai (2019)

directly through an increase in government spending is typically called expansionary or "loose." By contrast, fiscal policy is often considered contractionary or "tight" if it reduces demand through lower spending.[231]

The Republic of Guinea has a tax revenue of 12,201,000 USD made up of income taxes, value-added taxes, customs duties, taxes on capital gains, withholding taxes and cross-border taxes. In addition, it has a non-tax revenue of 704,000 USD; external revenue of 2,317,000 USD comes from aid and 1,625,000 USD from loans.[232] If one then tries, however, to link this fairly well detailed data to a budget policy, it is almost impossible to figure out what the country is seeking to do and how it intends to finance any changes being implemented through the budget.

Besides providing goods and services like public safety, highways, or primary education, fiscal policy objectives vary. In the short term, governments may focus on macroeconomic stabilization, for example, expanding spending or cutting taxes to stimulate an ailing economy, or slashing spending or raising taxes to combat rising inflation or to help reduce external vulnerabilities. If the long-term objective is to foster sustainable growth or reduce poverty, then there may be actions on the supply side to improve infrastructure or education.

Such objectives are broadly shared across countries, but their relative importance differs, depending on country circumstances. In the short term, priorities may reflect the business cycle, a response to a natural disaster, or a spike in food or fuel prices. In the long term, the drivers of fiscal policies can be development levels, demographics, or natural resource endowments. To reduce poverty, one approach could be to tackle looming long-term costs related to an aging population. In an oil-producing country, policymakers might try to better align fiscal policy with broader macroeconomic developments by moderating procyclical spending, both by limiting

---

[231] Bajpai (2019)
[232] Republic of Guinea (2017) p. 11

bursts of spending when oil prices rise and refraining from spending cuts when they drop.[233]

When spending cuts occur during a five-year development plan, the main foci of which is often industrialisation and human development. The plan fixes targets for growth in different sectors, control of HIV infections, enrolment in different educational systems, and the supply of other services such as water. Progress is assessed against the targets. These targets are reflected in the budget allocation.

In Tanzania, for example, about 22% of the budget excluding public debt service goes to education, 9.2% to healthcare, and 4.5% to the supply of water. Expenditures on peace and security operations are relatively low.[234] Military expenditure in Tanzania lies between 1.12% and 1.13% of the GDP, thus making Tanzania rank 88th out of 132 countries in terms of military spending.[235] This is low compared to, for example, South Sudan's 10.32% and the United States' 4.35%.

How do the percentages translate into Tanzanian shillings? In the first half of fiscal year 2016-2017, Tanzania spent 388.4 billion TZS on peace and security operations, but also a reasonable amount on free basic education, 124.9 billion TZS, and on healthcare services, 235.2 billion TZS. Development funds released to different authorities amounted to 1,608.6 billion TZS, which were used for the construction of roads, the supply of water, rural electrification, and the expansion of airports, among other purposes.[236] Data provided in percentages, if not seen next to the actual amount being spent, can obfuscate the fiscal ability of a state for the layperson and even for someone with a background in economics.

In Guinea, 8% of the revenues of the country are used to pay interest on debts. And 23% of the revenues are used for salaries and wages of officeholders and other agents of the state, like teachers, doctors, military personnel, and judges, that provide public services. Guinea spends 21% of the budget to buy goods and services, and

---

[233] Horton and El-Ganainy (2018)
[234] Republic of Tanzania (2016a) pp. 2 and 22
[235] CIA (2017a)
[236] CIA (2017b)

16% is used for subsidies and transfers. More than 30% of the budget is for investments. These expenditure categories and the corresponding percentage of the national budget spent on each is shown in Table 5. The budget covers diverse sectors such as rural development, infrastructure, social services, mines-energy-industry, and administration.

Table 5. Budget expenditure breakdown of Guinea, 2005-2015

Revenue	Percentage	Expenditure	Percentage
Tax	No policy	Debt interest	8
Debt	No ceiling	Recurrent expenditure	23
Aid	No ceiling	Goods and services	21
Business	No ceiling	Subsidies and transfers	16
		Investment	30
		Defence	2
		Total	**100**

Source: Republic of Guinea (2015)

The budget illustrated in Table 5 puts some emphasis on the development of the state through which it pursues the elimination of poverty. This approach led to the state's agricultural campaign of 2011-2012, which contributed to a 40% reduction in the 2007-2010 deficit of food self-sufficiency. On the other hand, the absence of electricity in certain regions led to a popular revolt.[237] There remains lack of clarity regarding the sources of revenue and regarding foregone revenue in the form of exemptions and incentives.

4.1.2. Budget functions

He who eats another man's food
will have his own food eaten by others.

Swahili proverb

---

[237] Ladepeche diplomatique (2013); Diallo (2017)

This section discusses three function of the budget: allocation of resources, distribution of resources, and stabilisation.

4.1.2.1. *Allocation function*

The allocation function as, a function of the budget, has to do with how resources are distributed and utilised. It presumes that an economy has a market mechanism that is well suited for the provision of private goods. The assumption is that the consumption of goods and services is based on exclusion unless you pay and is competitive. The government however is required to step in where the market cannot deal with a situation. This turns the allocation function into a political process. Voting by ballot replaces voting with money. Because voters know they will be subject to political decisions, they usually find it in their interest to vote, so that the outcomes of decisions fall closer to their preferences. Decision making by voting becomes a substitute for preference revelation through the market. If we say that social goods are provided publicly, it means that they are financed through the budget and made available free of charge. How these public goods and services are produced and their costs matter. We can look to the national accounts to discern the cost for the provision of goods through parastatals and state-owned enterprises and through national service systems, such as health and education. The provision and cost of services and goods is also in the salaries of public employees and purchases from private firms through public procurement processes. The public production of private goods should be carefully controlled and limited.

4.1.2.2. *Distribution function*

The distribution of resources is another function of the budget. This function is a major point of controversy in any budgetary debate, because it is operationalized through tax rates and transfer policies. In the absence of policy instruments, the distribution of income and wealth depends on the distribution of a person's earning ability which includes inherited wealth as well as salaries or wages. Concern for distribution appears to be shifting from relative income positions, the overall state of equality, and excessive income at the top of the scale to adequacy of income at the lower end. This is evident in discussions emphasizing the prevention of poverty and proposing a floor below which there can be no tax levied at the lower end.

Among various fiscal devices, redistribution is implemented most directly by:

- Tax transfer schemes, combining progressive taxation of high income with a subsidy to low-income households;
- Progressive taxes used to finance public services, which particularly benefits low-income households; and
- A combination of taxes on goods purchased largely by high income consumers with subsidies for other goods which are used chiefly by low-income consumers.

4.1.2.3. Stabilisation function

Stabilisation does not come automatically but requires policy guidance.[238] Without it, the economy tends to be subject to substantial fluctuations, and with growing international interdependence, forces of instability may be transmitted from one country to another, which further complicates the problem. The overall levels of employment and of prices in the economy depend upon the level of aggregate demand, relative to potential or capacity output valued at prevailing prices. The level of demand is a function of the spending decisions of millions of consumers. These decisions in turn depend on many factors, such as past and present income, wealth position, credit availability, and expectations. In any one period, the level of expenditures may be insufficient to secure full employment of labour and other resources. Expansionary measures to raise aggregate demand are then needed. Expenditures may also exceed the available output under conditions of high employment and thus may cause inflation. In such situations, restrictive measures are needed to reduce demand.

Policy measures available to deal with these problems involve both monetary and fiscal measures.

- Monetary instruments. If left to its own devices, the banking system will not generate precisely that money supply which is compatible

---

[238] Musell (2009)

with economic stability but will accentuate prevailing tendencies to fluctuation. The money supply must be controlled by the central banking system and be adjusted to the needs of the economy in terms of both short-term stability and long-range growth.[239]

- Monetary policy. Cash ratios, treasury bills, discount rates, interest rates, exchange rates, etc. are an indispensable component of stabilization policy. Expanding money supply will tend to increase liquidity, reduce interest rates, and thereby increase the level of demand, with monetary restriction working in the opposite direction.

- Fiscal instruments. An increase in public expenditures will be expansionary because demand is increased, initially in the public sector, and then the increase in demand is transmitted to the private market. Tax reduction, similarly, may be expansionary because taxpayers are left with a higher level of income and may be expected to spend more. Expansionary effects of deficit finance, if matched by a tight monetary policy, will call for an increase in the rate of interest.[240]

In Tanzania, food prices increased heavily in early 2017, due to a long drought. In local markets, foodstuff like maize and millet sold at two times the prices of the previous year, making it nearly impossible for some families to buy food. There seemed to be no intervention on food prices, although this is important for the stability of the economy. Combined with the low income of most people, this *laissez-faire* approach can be problematic.[241]

4.2. Guiding principles of fiscal systems

The principles of fiscal systems are criteria for classifying policy considerations but are not complete in themselves. Decisions on revenue and expenditure involve trade-offs,[242] and hence political or value judgements. There is no unique technically correct solution. There are no clear principles on aid, loans, trade or government business, but principles of taxation are fairly clearly defined. It has been argued that the tax system in order to achieve certain objectives

---

[239] IMF (2019a)
[240] Bajpai (2019); IMF (2014) p. 5
[241] IPS (2017)
[242] an exchange that occurs as a compromise

chooses and adheres to certain principles, which are termed its characteristics.[243]

A good tax system, therefore, is one designed based on an appropriate set of principles. However, tax objectives conflict with each other, and there is usually a need for compromise.[244]

The principles of taxation are traceable to the 10th century African philosopher Ibn Khaldun. He was the first to lay down the principles or canons of taxation. Based on the assumption that no one likes to pay taxes, Ibn Khaldun argued for low tax rates so that the incentive to work is not killed, and taxes are paid willingly. This principle was later set out by David Ricardo[245] and reiterated by Stiglitz[246] and has since been referred to as the canon of justice. It is an overarching principle that Ibn Khaldun argued should guide all fiscal decision making. Justice, one of the elements of fiscal legitimacy discussed in Chapter 2, builds a better understanding between the state and society.

However, most countries in the world including African countries, base their economies on the same principles but as laid down by Adam Smith in *Wealth of Nations*.[247] Smith's first rule was that any tax should be related to the ability to pay, provided that it does not become a disincentive to further work or capital accumulation. It is my contention that the "ability to pay" principle is being defeated, and taxation is instead serving at the very basic level to increase poverty. Ibn Khaldun, in discussing the ability to pay of taxpayers argued that when government is honest and people-friendly, "taxation yields a large revenue from small assessments."[248] However, this also touches upon Smith's canon of economy which recommends that the cost of collecting tax should be the minimum that is possible for both the government and the taxpayer.

The Republic of Somalia, grappling with civil war, fails to redistribute income, because taxes within the country are rare.

---

[243] Waris (2007) p. 274
[244] Waris (2007) p. 276
[245] Ricardo and Sraffa (1962)
[246] Stiglitz (2014)
[247] Smith (1977/1776)
[248] Khaldun (1377)

Remittances help to reduce the poverty, but 51.6% of the Somali population still lives below the poverty line. On the other hand, Puntland, a more developed region within the country, set the first income tax bracket at 22 USD of income per year; at a rate of 2%, the tax is 88 cents or less than 1 USD, which it not a heavy burden. The government, thus, does not push the population down by heavily taxing the poor but rather ensures they are within a tax bracket and uses other means to develop the region, i.e. taxing the richer part of the population at a high rate.

In Tanzania, on the other hand, income tax has five categories, and taxation is progressive as income rises. The first rate of 10% starts at a yearly income of 1,200,000 TZS or 530 USD, which is about 1.50 USD of income a day. Thus, taxpayers earning approximately 45 USD a month pay approximately 4 USD per month in taxes, a fairly high amount. This creates an incentive for people to avoid paying taxes by staying out of formal structures, which can counter the development of an efficient fiscal system.[249]

The principle of John Locke, echoed by the French philosophers of the 18th century, is that man is entitled to the fruits of his labour.[250] That leads to the clear philosophical belief that it is a contradiction in a free society for government to take more than half the fruits of a man's labour.

Does the government of a people today have a right to take compulsorily more than one third of the fruits of a man's labour in a developing country? Progressive 18th century thinkers such as Locke[251] and Hume[252] would have found this to be wrong. In many African countries, however, it is argued that the government collects more that 50% of the total earnings of a person through diverse taxes including but not limited to personal income tax, VAT, customs and excise duties, transaction taxes, and levies for petroleum, development funds, and capital gains.

If we cannot take more than a certain percentage of revenue from a taxpayer, then it is a principle that taxation should never be used as

---

[249] Republic of Tanzania (2016b)
[250] Locke (1690) chapter 5 section 27
[251] Locke (1690)
[252] Hume (1748)

a tool for social engineering. Designing a tax specifically to achieve a social purpose, which is the case of the "sin taxes," is, arguably, not merely economically inefficient but can also be socially divisive. The new taxes on social media usage in Uganda are a form of social engineering. Government spending is as well, however, because its whole purpose is to redistribute wealth and help those unable to help themselves for a period of time or perpetually. Government must also finance the defence of the realm and afford protection to the poorest in society.

Another principle upon which taxation is based was abundantly clear 200 years ago but has been truly noticed again only in the past 20 to 30 years. That principle is that no country can afford to enter on its own a *cul de sac* of taxation quite separate from the systems of its neighbours. No open and free trading society, such as Kenya, can adopt a taxation system removed from that of its neighbours and competitors, hence the creation of the East African Community and the Common Market for Eastern and Southern Africa as well as other African regional economic bodies. A country cannot go in a different direction from that taken by societies similar to its own. It may be thought that taxation can be dragged in one direction or another, but no society can afford to march in a direction different from that taken by history, neighbours, friends and competitors.

That goes against the concept that tax should be linked to ability to pay. In a modern society, as illustrated by the approach in Tanzania, income tax is no longer the fairest way of raising income.[253] The idea that income tax hits the rich harder than the poor is also untrue. Thomas Piketty, a French economist, presents a wealth tax as being a well targeted way to reduce inequality.[254] It would supposedly take from the very rich without hurting the poor or middle class. One of the surprises of the quantitative analysis, however, is that it would make everyone poorer.[255] The notion that income is the only way of achieving graded collection of taxation is out of date. Because we are now live in consumer societies, and the

---

[253] Fabian Society (2000)
[254] Fox (2015)
[255] Schuyler (2014)

spread of wealth throughout society has taken that form, the fairest taxes that are most directly linked to ability to pay are those on luxury or non-essential items, not only general income taxes.

The dynamism of the tax system is important for developing economies; the structure and rates of tax must be constantly the reviewed.[256] A good tax system should run in harmony with society. Government should set out national objectives that reflect societal requirements and assist a society in developing and in alleviating poverty. It should accommodate the attitude, problems and context of all taxpayers without losing sight of the administrative practicability or the goals of social and economic justice. The system chosen should result in the collection of adequate revenue for state expenses and development while remaining flexible enough to work with the changing requirements of the state, the people and the national, regional and global economy.

A good tax system recognises the basic rights of taxpayers.[257] A taxpayer is expected to pay taxes but not be harassed, hence, tax laws should be in simple language, and tax liability should be determinable with certainty. The mode and timings of payment should accommodate the taxpayer to the greatest extent possible. At the same time, a tax system should be equitable and progressive. Manifestos on taxpayer rights, to assist in achieving these characteristics, are proliferating.

Developed free market economies are subject to cyclical fluctuations; a good tax system should be flexible enough to counteract this. All possible sources of savings and capital accumulation should be explored. Lack of private savings and investments necessitates greater reliance on budgetary savings at the main source of capital accumulation. The private sector and the tax system should encourage customers and taxpayers to purchase durable consumption goods. Heavy import duties should be used to curb the import of luxury items, thus curbing the demand for such items, to focus on the efficiency of the production of other goods, including those important for food security.

---

[256] Nantob (2014)
[257] Cadesky, Hayes and Russell (2016)

Another problem that developing economies in Africa face is that of regional disparities. Tax measures should be devised to counteract this tendency and bring about more equitable economic growth. Growth or depressions as well as conflicts can result in inflation, deflation or collapses of an economy, and these should be at minimum recognised and where possible corrected and resolved.[258]

Ibn Khaldun, Smith, Ricardo and Stiglitz elaborated these fiscal principles. Smith believed that the private sector was more efficient than the public sector and that the prime responsibility of economic growth should be vested in the private sector. These principles or canons[259] have a philosophy behind them and exhibit an insight into the practical aspects of tax administration and its effects. However, in view of developments in economic philosophy and problems of the modern state, a few additional principles have been suggested by later writings. The first four principles were articulated by Ibn Khaldun and Adam Smith and the remainder by various other scholars.

4.2.1. Canon of equality or equity

One person is a thin porridge;
two or three people are a lump of ugali.

Kuria proverb

The subjects of every state ought to contribute towards the support of the government, as nearly as possible, in proportion to their respective abilities, that is, in proportion to the revenue which they respectively enjoy under the protection of the state.[260]

The canon of equality or equity concerns economic justice. The state allows for the earning and enjoying of extra income, however, the richer should pay more taxes. This principle has three limbs. Horizontal equity: People in equal circumstances should pay equal amounts of tax. Vertical equity: People with different scales of income must be treated differently. Benefits equity: Those who

---

[258] Shere (1948)
[259] Smith (1977/1776) called these principles canons of taxation.
[260] Smith (1977/1776) book 5, chapter 2, part 2

obtain more benefits from government should pay more tax. However, this third concept, of benefits, needs to be fully understood and nuanced, as does its application.[261]

The application of the canon of equality or equity can support or penalise the poor and vulnerable and must be carefully thought through. According to Ibn Khaldun, justice should not be limited to issues of the economy but include social justice as well.

4.2.2. Canon of certainty

The tax each individual is bound to pay ought to be certain, and not arbitrary. The time of payments, the manner of payments, and the quantity to be paid ought all to be clear and plain to the contributor, and to every other person. Taxpayers should not be subject to the arbitrariness and discretion of tax officials, because that breeds a corrupt tax administration.

Several factors make a tax certain. First, the timing of the tax must be known in advance. Second, the place of payment must be known. Third, the amount due must be known in advance. Fourth, the reason for payment must be clear; there can be no tax without law, and there must be a reason for it, e.g. raising government revenue. Finally, the form of payment must be known, i.e. what legal tender is required. In the past, this was taken in kind. Now we use legal tender. Revisions to tax schemes are made annually. Cross-border tax processes take longer to negotiate; formulas for a small percentage increase in the tax after a fixed period or a decrease based on the growth of the economy may be a solution.

4.2.3. Canon of convenience

According to the canon of convenience, the mode and timings of tax payment should be, as far as possible, convenient to the taxpayer. The collection systems in place should reflect taxpayer and state circumstances.

---

[261] See "The principle of equity in taxation – explained!" Accessed 6 October 2019. www.yourarticlelibrary.com/economics/taxation/the-principle-of-equity-in-taxation-explained-2/38118

4.2.4. Canon of economy

According to the canon of economy, the cost of the collection of tax should be the minimum possible both to the government and the taxpayer. It is useless for government to impose taxes if they are too difficult and costly to administer, which would also be burdensome to society. Thus, there is need for good administrative staff, up-to-date technology, and good rapport between government and the taxpayer. Stiglitz also refers to economic efficiency: the tax should allow for efficient allocation of resources.[262] In the context of health financing in Africa for example, efficiency could mean allocating 15% of the state budget to health as agreed by all African states in the Abuja Declaration. Coupled with transparency, this could result in a tax burden easily ascertainable and politically tailored to what society considers desirable.

4.2.5. Canon of productivity

Also called the canon of fiscal adequacy, the canon of productivity refers to the expectation that the tax system should be able to gain enough revenue for the treasury and government such that there should be no need to resort to deficit financing. Most states today work under deficit financing, and the use of deficits has resulted in differences in the debt burden of children. In the past five years, the debt burden in Kenya, for example, has grown from 800 USD for every child born to almost 1,500 USD, in contrast to Norway where every child born is a millionaire. However, the canon of productivity also assumes that a state must be capable of growth both in real and nominal terms, which means that growth should be visible and that the data should reflect the growth, including when it is not physically discernible. As years go by, revenues should increase so that revenues of any given year are more than those of the previous year.

---

[262] Stiglitz (2014)

4.2.6. Canon of buoyancy

We share the same sun but not our homes.

Kalenjin proverb

According to the canon of buoyancy, the tax revenue should have an inherent tendency of increasing along with the increasing national income, even if the rates and coverage of taxes are not revised.

4.2.7. Canon of flexibility

According to the canon of flexibility, it should be possible for authorities, without undue delay, to revise the tax structure, both with respect to its coverage and rates, to suit the changing requirements of the economy and of the treasury.[263] Funds must be redirected when necessary. In case of health emergencies, this should be carried out within certain parameters with minimum delay. For example, during maize shortages in Kenya, taxes were removed to stabilize prices and maintain food security. However, this itself is controversial, because VAT was never designed to be a tax on necessities but on luxuries. Another idea in this principle is that no tax should have such a large financial repercussion on the state resource purse that it creates fiscal instability.

4.2.8. Canon of simplicity

The tax system should not be too complicated, according to the canon of simplicity. It should be easy to understand and administer, and not breed problems of interpretation and legal disputes. To this Stiglitz[264] adds that the system should respond easily to changes in economic conditions. Simplicity, it is argued, is lost as society grows and the economy becomes complex, leading to "simplexity" as discussed in Chapter 5. For example, in 1973 when the Kenya Government took over its taxation matters from the East African Community (EAC), the income tax act was 11 pages. Today the same

---

[263] Blum (1976)
[264] Stiglitz (2014)

act is more than 15 times longer. The US income tax act is 12 volumes of over 4,000 pages.

Figure 11. Images from Guinea's citizen guides on the national budget[265]

In 2017, the Guinean government inaugurated a citizen guide to help in understanding the annual budget of the nation (see images from the 2017 and 2019 guides in Figure 11). With this guide, the government tries to give more publicity to the revenues and expenditures of the state and to inform people about the process of the budget and the reasons to pay taxes. The budget can be found on Facebook and the website of the government. Data produced by all the structures of the national statistical system, the main indicators of socioeconomic development in Guinea, survey reports, and some databases can be found on website of the national institute of statistics of Guinea.[266]

---

[265] Republic of Guinea (2017) p. 9; Republic of Guinea (2019) pp. 1 and 7
[266] Republic of Guinea (2017, 2019); see also *Institut national de la statistique: des statistiques fiables pour la prise de décision*, www.stat-guinee.org

4.2.9. Canon of diversity

Tax revenue should not depend upon too few sources of public income, according to the canon of diversity. Such dependency would breed uncertainty for the treasury. If tax revenue comes from diversified sources, then a reduction in one tax revenue stream will not upset the overall budget. However, the multiplicity of taxes must also be avoided, so as not to generate unnecessary costs of collection, which would violate the canon of economy. Diversity, argued Stiglitz,[267] requires that there be diverse sources of state income, not just taxation but other forms of revenue from investments, state-owned enterprises as well as natural resource rent.

4.3. Exceptions to fiscal principles

4.3.1. Constitutional, legislative and policy exceptions

The law requires all resources to be collected, but most countries put in additional laws to give different forms of preferential treatment to different sectors of the society, to achieve their diverse policy objectives like alleviation of poverty, encouraging investment, or even economic diversification. However, data on the exemptions and the value of government revenue forgone as a result of them remains inaccessible across the continent, with only piecemeal data available at a country-by-country level.

Tanzania, for example, grants a lot of exemptions to privileged groups. The government has established Special Economic Zones (SEZs) to promote rapid economic growth by attracting investments and technology through fiscal and business incentives. Article 28 of the Special Economic Zones Act provides for a range of tax exemptions. The SEZs include ICT parks, science and technology parks, free ports,[268] tourism development zones, and Export Processing Zones (EPZs). In EPZs, companies enjoy n wide range of tax exemptions. An example is the exemption from any payment of corporate tax for an initial period of 10 years, which explains why a mining company in Tanzania changes its name every ten years.

---

[267] Stiglitz (2014)

[268] A free port is a special economic zone encompassing an entire port area.

Other exemptions include remission of customs duties, VAT, and any other tax charges on raw materials and capital goods related to production in the EPZs, exemption from payment of all taxes and levies imposed by local authorities, and the list goes on.[269] All kinds of sectors can be involved, like agriculture, mining, metal production, light industries, electronics, etc. Furthermore, there is a general VAT relief to mining, oil and gas.[270] Ghana, on a different trajectory, is working toward an inclusive green economy with principles of sustainable banking, and perhaps there is need for some reflection on the position in Tanzania

4.3.2. Contractual and debt obligations

Stability clauses have a bad reputation and for good reason. Put into state and business contracts, they state that any changes in law made after the contract is signed will not be applicable to the contracting parties. Such provisions undermine the sovereignty of the state and promote "mischief" in relation to the law. Granting any taxpayer party the power to avoid the laws of the state is discriminatory against people and society.

Debt similarly tends to have conditions, imposed by organizations such as the IMF, but any conditions that affect the independence of a state in making the decisions it sees best for its people undermine governance and sovereignty as well as the taxing rights of the state.

4.3.3. Treaty obligations

According to a report from Action Aid, Senegal is offering lots of tax incentives to investors, like reduced corporate tax rates or even certain periods of time without tax. Senegal tries to attract foreign direct investment to the country in this way, and, according to Action Aid, the country loses a lot of possible tax revenue and without the projected job and employment increases. Such incentives cause a race

---

[269] Republic of Tanzania (2017a) articles 21 and 28
[270] Republic of Tanzania (2017b) and Republic of Tanzania (2017c)

to the bottom among West African states and could be destructive for their tax revenues.[271]

In Senegal, there is a special tax regime for approved export firms. When they export more than 80% of their turnover, the corporate tax is only 15%. The standard CIT is 30%. They also are entitled to some exemptions like no customs duties for utilitarian and tourism vehicles and for vehicles used for the transport of the productions, no tax on salaries, no registration duties, no patent fees, no property tax, and no tax on incomes on stocks and shares. When companies can prove the export is effective and the revenues get repatriated back to Senegal, they are allowed to reduce their taxable income by 50%. Companies in certain countries are privileged. Countries that have concluded a DTA with Senegal, where the tax rates of dividends, interest and royalties are negotiated, often have lower tax rates.[272]

Exemptions do attract investors, and governments claim that they bring more money into the country than is lost due to the exemptions. However, these exemptions destroy the taxation principles of equity and ability to pay. Indeed, it seems quite unfair that people living below the poverty line must pay taxes, whereas businesses making billions do not, which raises doubts as to the legitimacy of the fiscal and tax system.

4.4. Conclusion

The collection of state revenue has several objectives. The main ones follow. First, the collection of revenue is meant to maintain government. Second, it is important for the redistribution of income by taxing the wealth higher. Third, revenue helps clear market imperfections. Fourth, it stabilises the economy. Fifth, state revenue is collected to combat antisocial behaviour. Sixth, it is needed to implement government policy. Finally, revenue collected by the state is used to moderate social variances within society to enable the poor to live a life of material dignity, by spending more on them,

---

[271] Action Aid (2015)
[272] KPMG (2016) p. 4

subsidising services and goods they receive, or granting them exemptions and incentives.

The main challenges in each country vary, but all countries need to promote economic growth, monitor incidents of absolute and relative poverty, ensure stability of income and employment, and fight chronic unemployment, often tied to regional disparities.

The tax system must be politically acceptable and in conformity with the administrative capabilities of the authorities. However, there is inevitable conflict between defined policies and the ability to execute them, and taxes often tend to work at cross purposes. Equity and resource mobilisation considerations dictate what the tax burdens are and how they are distributed among sectors and among individuals.

Taxation should be guided by an overall principle of justice in addition to balancing out the principles or canons of equity, certainty, convenience, economy, productivity, buoyancy, flexibility, simplicity, and diversity Taxation should be progressive, not burdensome, and disfavour the tax evader. Rates should be moderate. Exorbitant tax rates disfavour earnings from savings and create a black money economy.

Chapter 5

Makers, Implementers and Interpreters of Fiscal Law and Policy

When a fire starts from the shrine,
no precaution can be possible.

Proverb from Uganda

The spirit of the law and its interpretation are crucial in understanding any law in a country. In fiscal and tax law, the debates tend to circle around whether tax is "simple" or "complex."[273] At the end of the day, any legal system, depending on the number of laws, clarity of terms, level of knowledge of the population, and numerous other factors, can result in an interpretation of a law that can go from simple to complex. Fiscal law and tax law are well known for the large amount of legislation and the complexity in its interpretation. Some scholars question whether simplification is even practical.[274] Simplification, it is argued, could reduce or increase fairness.[275] In some countries like Australia, the income tax regulations alone are over a thousand pages in length[276] or the height of a 10-year-old child.

Efforts to simplify tax and fiscal law may lead to a phenomenon known as "simplexity." According to various authors, the use of plain language to explain complex tax and fiscal rules and regulations often yields "simplexity," which occurs when clear and simple explanations of the law are provided, but they do not highlight the underlying complexities.[277] Simplexity may give rise to unequal outcomes for the taxpayer, and in most cases, arguably, the sophisticated taxpayer will bear the lowest cost.[278]

---

[273] Tickle (2018)
[274] See McCaffery (1990)
[275] Simon (1987)
[276] This is only a rough estimate gained from an examination of the all the tax laws and regulations reprinted by government printers in Kenya. These volumes are not consecutively paginated, making a precise count difficult.
[277] Blank and Osofsky (2017)
[278] Blank and Osofsky (2017)

Law, and by extension fiscal and tax law, at minimum, consists of a constitutional basis, legislation, and policy. This is not unusual for any law. The additional challenges with tax and fiscal laws, however, are that a finance bill with amendments is passed annually, government policies change with each successive national election, and responses to changing economic and technological circumstances accumulate rapidly. Thus, tax and fiscal laws quickly become defunct and also result in some of the most voluminous legislation.

Whether complicated rules enhance fairness rests on whether the tax rules are utilised to determine all tax outcomes. However, the question of legal determinacy has been a subject of controversy for decades[279] and continues as a topic of debate in legal scholarship.[280] To the extent law is indeterminate, it cannot ensure fairness, because it is not the law that decides the outcome.[281] To the extent law is determinate, there may still be no guarantee of fairness, if it can only be determinate by being arbitrary.

In this chapter, to better understand fiscal and tax law and the work of its makers, implementers, and interpreters, after a discussion of the indeterminacy of the law and the philosophy of government, the chapter will explore the social context approach to rulemaking and the elaboration approach. Those who opt for the elaboration approach towards tax rulemaking believe they have found a safe passage between arbitrariness and indeterminacy. Then we will further explore the debate about the indeterminacy of tax law and contrast principle vs. rules-based legislation.

---

[279] Frank (1936); Fuller (1958); Llewellyn (1960)
[280] Cornell (1988); Hart (1994)
[281] If law is indeterminate, it should not prevent fairness either.

5.1. Practical and theoretical indeterminacy of law

If you visit the home of the toads, stoop.

Anang proverb

In all areas of law there are at least two categories of legal indeterminacy, practical indeterminacy and theoretical indeterminacy.[282] Practical indeterminacy recognizes that the application of law to facts is complicated and therefore requires some discretion or interpretation, which may change the result. Practical indeterminacy is the recognition of the power of judges to create different outcomes through the manner in which they frame the issues and find or omit the facts, a common law phenomenon in former British colonies that is not as prevalent among civil law jurisdictions often former Dutch, French, Portuguese or Spanish colonies.

Theoretical indeterminacy, in contrast, does not derive simply from human frailty or corruptibility but from the difficulties inherent in the use of language and in the intervention of human perception between law and reality. The theory of legal indeterminacy holds that the law does not mandate a single outcome in any given case,[283] and this results in precedent setting, common in former British colonies. This means a case decided by a judge, for instance, could be rightly decided for both parties within the confines of the law. Because 50% of African countries follow a common law system, this means that most practice precedent setting, in a spirit of legal and practical indeterminacy, as described by Miller[284]. Note that precedent-setting legal systems in Africa predated colonial rule, dating back to ancient Egypt and to a thousand years ago in the Horn of Africa.

Taken to the extreme, the belief in theoretical indeterminacy would lead one to conclude that law never determines outcomes in cases.[285] Civil law systems have extensive codes, however, the result is that if there is an absence of a specific provision, then there is no

---

[282] Endicott (1996) p. 669
[283] Kress (1989)
[284] Miller (1993) p. 10
[285] D'Amato (1989)

room for the judge to exercise law-making power. All former French, Portuguese, and Belgian colonies still use this system, except for Rwanda which has adopted precedent making. Burundi, as a member of the East African Community (EAC), should also be making changes to its laws to follow the precedent-setting system, in a spirit of legal and practical indeterminacy.

Tax complexity has many faces.[286] It can be examined from various perspectives, including those of the taxpayer, the government, the return preparer, the planner, and the scholar. Any attempt to categorize tax complexity is likely to be fundamentally arbitrary. The various categories of complexity one might derive are likely to overlap and interrelate in a fashion that renders separate treatment difficult and of limited value. So, let us consider elaborative complexity and judgmental complexity. Elaborative complexity relates to the level of information and education that must be absorbed o begin to decide a tax question. The length and detail of tax rules, along with their interconnectedness, are directly related to their elaborative complexity. Judgmental complexity refers to the intellectual, moral, and philosophical burdens a tax question may pose for one who has mastered the rules.[287]

5.2. Philosophy of government

> *To love the king is not bad,*
> *but a king who loves you is better.*
>
> Wolof proverb

With every new political administration comes the philosophy and accompanying policies of the party or parties in power. If the philosophy is clear, then so is the way forward for the electoral cycle – often of five years, as in Kenya and South Africa, or seven years, as in Rwanda and Senegal. With coalitions and with ethnic-based politics, however, comes more uncertainty in the legal and fiscal system, because a system of favours and compromises is operative

---

[286] D'Amato (1989)
[287] McCaffery (1990) and Partlow (2013) p. 307

almost daily and leads to even more uncertainty for those outside the circles of the political elite.

Despite uncertainties, the sources of law provide a foundation for interactions and interpretation. In common law countries like Ghana, Uganda, and Kenya, the domestic sources of law are the constitution, treaties, legislation, case law, regulation, and, finally, academic texts and best practice.[288] International sources of law include: *jus cogens*, treaties, custom, state practice, and academic text.[289] Other African countries such as Gabon and Algeria follow the civil law system. Others, including South Africa, use a combination of both civil and common law regimes. Understanding and interpreting domestic law can be rather straightforward, however, the use of international materials in domestic interpretation causes great difficulty, especially in the case of legal indeterminacy.

5.3. The rule maker and the planner of laws

> *Advice is a stranger. If he's welcome,*
> *he stays for the night; if not, he leaves the same day.*
>
> Malagasy proverb

Let us draw on Miller[290] who describes how tax thought is embodied in two hypothetical individuals, the rule maker and the planner. "The rule maker seeks symmetry and wholeness in the law." He or she is the parliamentarian passing legislation and the civil servant drafting legislation for parliament to create the legal fiscal system or negotiating tax treaties. "The planner seeks certainty and narrow truth."

> The taxation process in which both the rule maker and the planner participate begins with the making of the rule imposing the tax. The planner responds with a variety of manoeuvres ranging from compliance to open challenge. Usually, the planner's preferred course of action is to devise a strategy that deflects the force of the rule without questioning its legitimacy. In other words, the planner tries to get outside the rule. But in so doing the

---

[288] Hoffman and Rumsey (2012) p. 3
[289] United Nations (1945) article 38
[290] Miller (1993) p. 13

planner will seek to allow the taxpayer to persist in the economic substance of the activity that is the intended target of the tax.[291] [292]

This gap is filled by government administrators, such as revenue officials in the treasury and the ministry finance as well as the revenue authority itself and the drafters of the budget including the Attorney General's office.[293]

Loans from institutions like the IMF have conditionalities regarding economic and fiscal policy and more often tax policy.[294] Senegal for example is a member of AFRITAC West, an organization under the wings of the IMF that helps member states by giving technical advice in core microeconomic and financial management areas.[295] The result is that most African countries do not have independently developed tax policies. There is need for clarity on policy, relations, the size of the economy, and tax rates. Understanding of policy and cost-benefit analysis should precede negotiations. However, negotiators are often called for right before the crossing of borders to sign agreements. Negotiators are often put on planes and forced to negotiate at the last minute. In the absence of a clear philosophy and clear policy, these types of political manoeuvres are inescapable.

The result is the inevitable loss of the right to tax: taxing right. Negotiators then demand terms that are unobtainable, to block the treaty. States are now trying to organize better for state visits, however, coordination is informal and not based on policy. Ghana and South Africa have policies about negotiation processes. Those in South Africa are more detailed and contextualised. A parliamentary committee reviews tax treaties before their ratification in parliament.

---

[291] "This effort to skirt the law and the response it draws from the rule maker is the chief systemic cause of complexity. *See* McCaffery [1990], *supra* note 19 at [pp.] 1275-76. This 'dynamic' complexity may be viewed as an inevitable cyclical phenomena of tax law. When the level of complexity reaches the point when it is no longer tolerable, it is time for volcanic upheaval in the form of a tax reform act that so radically alters the legal landscape as to render much of the previous gamesmanship irrelevant. *Id.* at [pp.] 1277-79." Miller (1993) p. 13

[292] Miller (1993) p. 13

[293] Miller (1993) p. 13

[294] Eurodad (2006) pp. 3 and 15

[295] IMF (2019a)

In Kenya, tax treaties go to the executive rather than the parliament, and a minister signs off on them. As a result, there is no democratic oversight, and competent authority becomes a contestable issue. The treaty ratification act does not include tax treaties.

What about multilateral tax treaties? In Kenya, citizens are given a relief of credit if they paid taxes in another country. Tax rates are normally policy, but treaties arguably bring stability. However, guarantees of capital and fair judiciaries are considered more important. A multilateral treaty with tax implications is AfCFTA. A new type of treaty being developed at the OECD is called the Multilateral Instrument (MLI).[296] The MLI is very dense and holds many options. The MLI pertains to all treaties in the world, but each set of two bilateral states has to agree to amend existing treaties clause by clause.

The biggest challenge is no longer capacity but data and its ability to inform policy choices. In the absence of a clear cost-benefit analysis, negotiators are unaware of their own power. When unaware of the number of MNEs in their country, they are not in a position to negotiate strategically.

Tax treaties between two countries are only of value after there is enough business between the two countries. In Table 6 is a list of African countries and the number of double tax agreements DTAs they had in place as of 2018.

Table 6: Number of double tax agreements (DTAs) in African countries

Country	Number of DTAs	Country	Number of DTAs	Country	Number of DTAs
Algeria	29	Gabon	5	Nigeria	15
Angola	0	Ghana	8	Rwanda	2
Benin	2	Gambia	0	São Tomé and Príncipe	0
Botswana	6	Guinea	1	Senegal	14
Burkina Faso	2	Guinea Bissau	0	Seychelles	14

---

[296] OECD (2016a)

Country	Number of DTAs	Country	Number of DTAs	Country	Number of DTAs
Burundi	0	Kenya	12	Somalia	0
Cameroon	4	Lesotho	3	South Africa	58
Cape Verde	1	Liberia	4	South Sudan	0
Central African Republic	0	Libya	12	Sudan	11
Chad	1	Malawi	8	Swaziland	5
Comoros	1	Mali	2	Tanzania	8
Congo Brazzaville	0	Mauritania	2	Togo	2
Cote d'Ivoire	10	Mauritius	44	Tunisia	0
Democratic Republic of Congo	3	Morocco	47	Uganda	10
Egypt	49	Mozambique	5	Zambia	21
Equatorial Guinea	0	Namibia	8	Zimbabwe	14
Eritrea	1	Niger	1		
Ethiopia	9				

Source: Author

Several questions arise from this picture of African countries with DTAs. Why do these countries have DTAs with certain other countries? Is there enough business between each set of two countries to justify the continued existence of the DTA? Why is existing domestic legislation not adequate to prevent double taxation, thus avoiding costly and time-consuming negotiations that are susceptible to lobbying and power imbalances?

What is also unclear is why African countries use model treaties instead of individually tailored approaches based on economic activity. DTA models of the UN and OECD are guidelines and not starting and endpoints. The African Tax Administration Forum (ATAF), ECOWAS, COMESA, and SADC also have model DTAs, but even these have provisions not always to the benefit of developing countries. This discussion of DTAs highlights the need to ensure appropriate legislation is in place and then when necessary negotiate and sign onto treaties. The rule maker and the planner come into play, and in the case of multilateral treaties, the negotiator as well.

5.3.1. Social context approach to rule making

Miller[297] explains how the rule maker anticipates "that the planner will seek to get outside the rule" in imposing the tax, which is legal but explores and often exploits loopholes in the law. This is frequent in the UK and in other countries that practice common law. By introducing a piece of legislation that introduces penalties for tax avoidance, for example in Kenya's Tax Procedures Act of 2015[298], does the rule maker limit the taxpayer's options for exploiting loopholes in the law?

One approach of the rule maker is to:

> write the rule in broad terms so as to cast a net around all economically similar activities no matter the form in which they are carried out. This is called the social context approach because it asks those who apply the law to look beyond the rule itself for its proper application and to focus instead on the social justice of taxing particular transactions in particular fashions. The social context approach asks that laws be applied in accordance with their purposes, and, consequently, regards law itself as something more than duly promulgated written rules. It is an approach that is thoroughly consonant with the internal morality of tax law as viewed from the rule maker's perspective.[299]

In Kenya's current 2010 constitution, the discussion of principles of taxation is a direct reflection of an attempt by the rule maker (society through the national constitutional conference and referendum) to clarify and guide the roles and products of planners and other rule makers, prioritising clearly the social context

---

[297] Miller (1993) p. 16
[298] Republic of Kenya (2015)
[299] Miller (1993) p. 16

approach.[300] The Rwandan constitution also adopts this approach,[301] as do the constitutions of Morocco and South Africa.

In Uganda, the rule maker has gone further to provide rules to guide its role. The Ugandan Tax Procedures Code Act of 2014[302] was enacted with the aim of harmonising and consolidating the procedural rules for the administration of tax laws in Uganda, and for connected purposes. The Act, which is supposed to bring about efficiency and effectiveness in tax collection and compliance, may not achieve its objective. Just like other tax laws, this Act has been criticised by legal practitioners and tax experts alike. Kenya, in 2015 also enacted a Tax Procedures Act.[303]

Some fear the new rules in these acts will interfere with the taxpayer's right to take advantage of tax laws.[304] In trying to balance between the taxpayer's rights and tax collection, courts (such as in the Bata case in Kenya[305]) have reiterated that payment of tax is an obligation imposed by the law and an involuntary activity. Therefore, a taxpayer is not obliged to pay more than is due to the tax collector.[306] The taxpayer's right to minimise his/her tax obligations, within the ambit of the law, emanates from this principle.

---

[300] Republic of Kenya (2010) article 209. Traditionally under case law, the judiciary and the tax administrators are required to read the law for the benefit of the taxpayer. It should at all times be maintained that as set out in **Khambaita v Commissioner of Income Tax** [1954] 21 EACA 16, the onus is on the taxpayer to show that the original assessment is excessive so that it is on the taxpayer to satisfy the High Court on any disputed issue. However, this must be tempered with the fact that in **Williamson v Commissioner of Income Tax** [1955] 22 EACA 227, the Commissioner must consider the company's position from a commercial point of view as a prudent person of business and not as a representative of the Government. This was clearly not done in the Khambaita case which should be read with section 123 of the Kenyan Income Tax Act (Republic of Kenya, 2012) which states that where there is uncertainty as to a question of fact or law, the commissioner has the discretion to refrain from assessing or recovering the tax in question.

[301] Republic of Rwanda (2003) chapter IX on State Finance and Taxes

[302] Republic of Uganda (2014)

[303] Republic of Kenya (2015)

[304] Rotuk (2016)

[305] Republic v Kenya Revenue Authority Exparte Bata Shoe Company (Kenya) Limited [2014] eKLR

[306] Republic v Kenya Revenue Authority Exparte Bata Shoe Company (Kenya) Limited [2014] eKLR

In the UK case of **Inland Revenue Commissioners v Duke of Westminster**,[307] the court was of the opinion that if there are two methods by which a transaction might be effected, which methods entail different tax consequences, the taxpayer may choose the method with lesser liability. In another UK case, of **W. T. Ramsay Limited v Inland Revenue Commissioner**,[308] the court emphasised that tax avoidance schemes are only tenable if they make commercial sense.

5.3.2. Elaboration approach to rule making

Miller[309] eloquently describes the elaboration approach to rule making, used especially in civil law systems, like in France and its former colonies such as Gabon and Algeria.

> ...the modern trend in rule making has been to set out the circumstances where the tax applies in minute detail. This is called the elaboration approach because it looks to the rules themselves for their proper application by specifying all the circumstances in which they apply. In its most elevated form, this approach is distinguished not only by the length of the rules but by their intricate interdependence. Often such rules cannot be applied by simply finding the single rule applicable to a given case. Instead, one must master all the rules to apply any one of them, because only mastery of all the rules will provide the answer to which rules apply.
>
> The elaborate architecture of these modern rules is due in part to their development by a handful of people over a limited time span. [...] The incrementalism [gradual change] characteristic of the social context approach is avoided to the extent such avoidance is practically possible. Because these rule makers are specialists they can make their rules quite elaborate while maintaining some degree of internal coherence. The goal of the rule makers is to anticipate all likely questions in advance of their arising. In this way, the elaboration approach seeks to adhere to the rule maker's broad conception of fairness while also being consonant with the planner's desire for certainty because it focuses on technical differentiation, completeness, and specificity.

Although this is not the current approach in most African countries, it could still be adopted. However, no bills on the African continent were following this approach as of July 2019.

---

[307] [1936] AC 1; 19 Tax Cases 490
[308] [1981] HL
[309] Miller (1993) p. 17

A side effect of the elaboration approach is to render the maneuvers of the planner less vulnerable to a contextual substance over form argument by the rule maker. Since the rule maker has chosen to detail her precise position, arguably she is obliged to live by her own rules to the letter. Moreover, it seems likely that courts will incline towards greater literalism in their interpretations of the rules in the face of such detailed analysis.[...] Thus, the elaboration approach to tax law is, in a sense, a capitulation to the moral perspective of the planner. The length and specificity of the rules is an implicit concession that the rules are everything; the rules are the whole law. If the literal language of a rule does not fit a transaction, that transaction is outside its application.[310]

In Kenya, in **Republic v Commissioner of Domestic Taxes (Large Taxpayers Office) Ex parte Barclays Bank of Kenya Limited**,[311] the court seemed to take this approach. Relying on a previous decision by Justice Nyamu in **Keroche Industries Limited v Kenya Revenue Authority & 5 Others**,[312] Justice Odunga stated:

In these kinds of cases therefore the Court is not entitled to attempt a discovery at the intention of the Legislature but is restricted to the clear words of the statute. In a taxing Act one has to merely look at what is clearly said since there is no room for any intendment. There is no equity about tax and there is no presumption as to tax. Nothing is to be read in, nothing is to be implied. One can only fairly look at the language used.

Miller continues:

If rules can be simultaneously determinate and fair, perhaps this capitulation to the planner's perspective is not a problem. If it is possible to achieve fair outcomes in a mechanical fashion, then literalism is not a hindrance to a sound tax system. On the other hand, if the elaboration approach overestimates or misunderstands the determinacy of rules and the connections between rules and fair outcomes, serious problems arise.[313]

In the latter case, the possibility of an unjust outcome arises for the taxpayer and the ability of the state to collect taxes could be diminished.

---

[310] Miller (1993) pp. 21-22
[311] [2015] cKLR
[312] [2007] eKLR
[313] Miller (1993) p. 22

5.3.3. The two approaches in contrast

Each approach to rule making – social context approach and elaboration approach – has its advantages and disadvantages. Miller[314] elaborates as follows:

> The social context approach can be brief and easily understood in outline, but it depends on a strong enforcement system and the willingness of judges to apply the law so as to treat matters that are similar in substance in the same way even if they are dissimilar in form. The social context approach is also incremental and evolutionary. Thus, it is subject to uncertainty and tends to encourage litigation. Because many of the judges upon which it depends are not tax specialists, the social context approach removes much authority over the sound administration of the tax system from the tax elite. It might be suggested that the social context approach lends itself to uninformed judicial meddling[315] and taxpayer abuse. Alternatively, one might characterize it as populist and as tending to inject an element of common sense into tax law.
>
> The elaboration approach, in contrast, seems to take away from judges the discretion to make bad decisions. However, its success depends upon the ability of the rule maker to be extremely foresighted in anticipating all the variations in form that an economically similar legal event might take (or be shaped to take by a clever planner). For this reason, the modern rules are often long, detailed, highly interwoven, and seek to address all possible contingencies. Viewed in a positive light, this approach uses great and fairminded elaboration to reduce the law to a series of mechanical rules whose application requires little or no human discretion to arrive at an outcome that treats all cases according to their substance.[...] From this reductionist perspective, the elaborative complexity of tax law is justified by its certain and uniform fairness when applied by one who has mastered it. Of course, mastery of the rules is rendered extremely difficult by their complexity and, thus, only an elite few will do so. This in itself might strike many as unfair.[...] But the deterministic fairness of the rules in the hands of one who has mastered them is seen (by those making the rules) to outweigh the unfairness proceeding from their complexity.[...] This rule-minded account of the operation of tax law seeks to make the law a precise and exacting tool for coordinating human activity.

In nations like those on the African continent this approach by Miller becomes of even more value as it allows for the capacity constraints to be resolved through better description of the legal provisions thus moving them away from complexity and more towards simplicity and

---

[314] Miller (1993) pp. 20-21

[315] "The nonspecialist judiciary is often considered an impediment to sound tax policy. For example, Professor James Eustice has called the Supreme Court a 'loose cannon on a rolling deck' in the field of tax." Eustice (1989) in Miller (1993) pp. 20-21.

allowing for simplexity to be the bridge that allows countries to better analyse and interpret fiscal laws.

5.4. Training of fiscal professionals

Instruction in youth is like engraving in stone.

Proverb from Morocco

Fiscal professionals globally and especially in developing countries do not necessarily choose their field as a first-choice profession. They come from completely diverse disciplines such as anthropology, geology or even veterinary sciences. Training comes from closely related fields like accounting and economics. As a result, the knowledge level of people in tax is varied and incomplete. Gaps on the continent include understanding of law and public finance, and development-oriented thinking and practice. Economists and accountants who provide training do not necessarily employ innovative approaches, integrate contextualized examples, or have deep understanding of systems that are societally centred.

Training on tax issues is provided in-house, by accounting firms or more recently through the revenue authority, or through international organizations. These approaches are problematic in that they are shaped by agendas and biases and deprive the sector of holistic training. This is potentially a problem not only in Africa but globally.

On issues of international and cross border tax, for example, the main trainers are from OECD, usually for the benefit of its 34 member states. ATAF trains on African issues and CIAT on Latin America issues, however, the training remains biased towards the bodies funding the organizations, and the consultant trainers often come from the global north. Some countries have specialized training centres for tax professionals, for example the Kenya School of Revenue Administration and the Chartered Institute of Taxation Ghana. There are also tax institutes and programmes in universities, such as the African Tax Institute at the University of Pretoria in South Africa and the tax talks as well as short courses run by the

Committee on Fiscal Studies at the Law School, University of Nairobi.[316]

5.5. To what extent is tax law indeterminate?

When trying to understand the roles of the makers, the planners and implementers, and the interpreters of fiscal and tax laws, one can already see that inconsistences in a fiscal system stem from them, as well as other stakeholders. In this section, we continue to draw on Miller and his exploration of the degree to which tax law is indeterminate and the "strengths and failings of rules."[317]

> The degree of indeterminacy of any particular area of law, such as tax, may be no different from the degree of indeterminacy of law generally. The jurisprudential scholars whose works are discussed here often seem to assume this.[318]

This section will unpack the additional layers that are specific to fiscal law and policy that show that indeterminacy in these areas is even greater and more of a challenge on the African continent. Legal indeterminacy has been divided into three categories:[319]

1. General legal indeterminacy: the meaning of the legal provision is subject to doubt;
2. Factual indeterminacy: the judge must find the facts to apply the positive law;
3. Mach/Fayerabend factual indeterminacy: the facts (or fact words) are dependent upon legal theory and special language.

The indeterminacy of fiscal or tax law (like other areas of law) resides in the fact that, despite elaborate rules, human judgement is still required to resolve complex situations.[320] Rules are nonetheless necessary, to provide clarity for all stakeholders and guide practice, including taxpayers themselves and also lawyers or accountants working for the best interests and outcomes for their clients.

---

[316] See https://cfs.uonbi.ac.ke
[317] Miller (1993) p. 24
[318] Miller (1993) p. 24
[319] Bogenschneider (2016); Miller (1993)
[320] Miller (1993) p. 78

5.5.1. The empirical evidence

How does one measure whether the law is clear enough for all the taxpayers? Could the measure be based on how few court cases are filed? "[S]ome commentators contend that the determinacy of law is proven by the number of cases that do not require litigation."[321] However, this stance does not account for lack of skills of revenue authority staff or even the fear of the tax collector. "The indeterminist response is to argue that the mere fact that most taxpayers do not end up before the tax court really tells us nothing."[322]

> Perhaps most returns just reflect one person's vision of what he should pay.[...] Perhaps enforcement is too lax. Perhaps most audited cases do not go to trial because the amount in controversy makes litigation not cost effective.[323]

Kenya has a population of approximately 44 million, a voter base of 18 million, and registered taxpayers amounting to 6 million, however only 2.6 million people paid their taxes on time in 2018. Tax literacy seems to pose a challenge in developing countries.[324]

In Namibia, which has a broad tax base, the Budget Highlights of March 2017 stipulated that there were some tax proposals to curb exemptions and deductions eroding the tax base. There is a proposal as well to adapt the provisions regarding the taxes on capital gains. They will be expanded to provide for wealth-based taxation of certain categories of capital assets, whilst now generally there is no tax on capital gains arising, or deemed to arise, from a source within Namibia.[325]

In the cases of Kenya and Namibia and many another African country, the nuances of the rules and the diverse situations of taxpayers strongly suggest contexts in which the law is indeterminate.

---

[321] Miller (1993) p. 24
[322] D'Amato in Miller (1993) p. 24
[323] Miller (1993) p. 24
[324] Waris (2014a)
[325] Ernst and Young (2017); Deloitte (2015); see also Deloitte (2017)

5.5.2. The easy tax case

Miller[326] presents a compelling argument about how tax law is indeterminate by discussing the easy case.

> Another way to examine tax indeterminacy that is closely related to the empirical approach is to consider the extent to which the easy case is the prevalent type of tax case. Those who believe law is largely determinate contend that there are many easy cases.[...] They say the only thing that prevents this fact from being readily apparent is that lawyers from their earliest training tend to focus on the hard cases[...]. In this context, the hard cases include all litigated cases. Lawyers never see most of the easy cases because they are never litigated.[327] [...]
>
> [T]wo cases are *never* precisely alike. That is one reason why law is indeterminate. In a world of infinite variety, no law can specify a single right outcome for any given case because no future case is an exact match for the lawmaker's paradigm case. [cited without the footnotes]

In the case of a taxpayer, because no employee and no businessperson operate in the same way, again, the possibilities and permutations of tax liability are of an unending variety. In most African countries, disputes are first negotiated to conclusion in confidentiality within the revenue authority, and often this is where most tax cases are resolved, especially in societies that do not have a tradition of being litigious or where there is fear of interaction with government.

This is particularly problematic in countries where corruption and the perception of corruption are high. Paying off revenue officials to finalise a case is often seen as more efficient for a taxpayer than going through the official process of dispute resolution.

Tax matters can be contested first administratively and then judicially. Taxpayers can file an objection to the assessment that has been made upon them by formulating it in writing and filing it with the Commissioner General. If not satisfied with the decision of the Commissioner General, the taxpayer can appeal to the "Board." From there an appeal can go to the Tribunal and again to the Court of Appeal, which is the highest court.

If there is not a separate tax court, it is likely that not all judges will fully understand the matters. In addition, some African countries

---

[326] Miller 1993 pp. 28 and 30
[327] Miller (1993) p. 28

have allowed tax matters to be managed by commercial courts which is not where they belong, single taxpayer cases are likely to be crowded out by cases with higher amounts at stake. What is needed is a separate tax court to handle all tax matters, no matter what their size, and divided into divisions based on types of taxes so that all are justly and equitably treated.

5.5.3. Problems with language and rules of interpretation

The four main rules of legal interpretation of all statutes must by necessity also apply to statutes dealing with finance and tax: the literal rule, the golden rule (used when the literal rule results in an absurdity), the mischief rule, and *ejus dem generis* (interpretation based on the context). These are the traditional rules of interpretation used by most African courts that follow the common law tradition. These rules, as applied to finance and tax, and additional considerations of language and interpretation are discussed in this subsection.

5.5.3.1. The indeterminacy of language makes literalism problematic

Understanding rules literally, simply by reference to the dictionary meanings of the words employed within them, raises the problem of the indeterminacy of language itself.

> That language communicates something is an inescapable conclusion. Even without the benefit of a particular context or the benefit of knowing the identity of the speaker, we gain more meaning from a sentence [... t]hough the meaning of any given word may change over time, still at any given moment in time any word will have some meaning that is widely accepted as inherent in that word.[...] When we have positive economic incentives for reading rules differently, it is likely we will seek out those different readings.[328]

5.5.3.2. Does the form-substance dichotomy leave room for mischief?

Miller[329] explores the form-substance dichotomy:

> Even when we can clearly distinguish substance from form, there remain competing pressures to honor both form and substance. Arguably, honoring the forms of transactions makes the law more predictable. Predictability is highly prized because it fosters stability and a sense of security. Not incidentally, it also opens the way for the planner to work his magic [or

---

[328] Miller (1993) pp. 34 and 37
[329] Miller (1993) p. 40

"mischief" of developing avoidance schemes]. Thus, on the other hand, it may be argued that taxing transactions according to their economic substance fosters fairness, and discourages manipulation of the form to obtain an advantage. Thus, the choice between taxing according to form or according to substance (if the two are seen as different) is a matter for judgment.

Common law systems should understand this to mean that any type of tax evasion counts as "mischief" not permitted under by taxation legislation.

5.5.3.3. The use of highly specific language

In, **Commissioner of Income Tax v Westmont Power**,[330] drawing on **Inland Revenue v Scottish Central Electricity Company**,[331] the court ruled as follows:

> Even though taxation is acceptable and even essential in democratic societies, taxation laws that have the effect of depriving citizens of their property by imposing pecuniary burdens resulting also in penal consequences must be interpreted with great caution. In this respect, it is paramount that their provisions must be express and clear so as to leave no room for ambiguity [...] any ambiguity in such a law must be resolved in favour of the taxpayer and not the Public Revenue Authorities which are responsible for their implementation.

In efforts to be clear, rule makers may want to use highly specific words or more words, which may add to the ambiguity of tax rules. Even in instances where tax officers see no ambiguity, disputes still arise regarding the interpretation of certain terms. In addition, a lay taxpayer does know have the same level of knowledge as a trained tax auditor or accountant. In **Republic v Commissioner of Domestic Taxes (Large Taxpayers Office) Ex parte Barclays Bank of Kenya Limited**,[332] a case concerning the interpretation of what constituted "Royalty payments and Management and Professional fees payments" Justice Odunga followed this line of thought in ruling in favour of the Applicant.

> A determinist might dismiss the foregoing examples by saying that of course there is some ambiguity and uncertainty inherent in our use of language but that nearly all such ambiguity can be overcome by the use of highly specific

---

[330] (K) Ltd [2006] eKLR
[331] [1931] 15 Tax Cases 761
[332] [2015] eKLR

definitions. However, this seems doubtful since we can only define words by the use of more words. The more words we define, the more words we are obliged to define, ad infinitum. In the end, even with all our specific rules and definitions we may still find that some uncertainties remain. Another problem that also arises [...] is the possibility that we will make a mistake because the rules are so complicated.[333]

5.5.3.4. The use of mathematical language

Students come to their first tax law class with a calculator, however, this is unnecessary. They need to understand overarching concepts of the legal framework, the contexts in which it is applied, and both its strengths and limits, rather than start by applying mathematical formulas. As Miller[334] points out, "Mathematical rules abound in tax law." He explains that they are part of the lengthy regulations that characterize the elaboration approach to rule making. Miller[335] elaborates:

> The unfairness of mathematical rules is not always so evident, but their essential feature is the failure to distinguish between individual circumstances in their application in a way that is more pronounced than other rules. In short, the mathematical rule is overtly arbitrary. This overt arbitrariness accounts for its relative determinacy. It also supports the idea that there is a correlation between arbitrariness and determinacy. The widespread use of the mathematical rule in tax law is probably the strongest point in favor of the contention that tax law is more determinate than law generally. [...] Mathematical rules may treat like cases alike but only on the basis of a narrow measure of likeness. For this reason individual fairness may be significantly lacking under a mathematical rule. Thus, heavy reliance on mathematical rules is likely to undermine the legitimacy of tax law.

In cases of transfer pricing, for example, in Kenya there are six formulas from which to choose. The taxpayer choice and the tax collector's questioning of the choice can result in indeterminacy, no matter what choice is made.[336]

> Tax language and, more generally, the English language[337] communicate shared meanings to those of us who employ them. These shared meanings allow us to employ language to constrain decisionmakers' choices in tax cases.

---

[333] Miller (1993) p. 40
[334] Miller (1993) p. 43
[335] Miller (1993) pp. 43-44
[336] Waris (2017a)
[337] And French, Arabic, Portuguese and Spanish for that matter (author addition)

However, language always poses problems for the administration of the tax laws no matter how one attempts to use it. If we use broad terms, the statute is ambiguous on its face. Even if we use terms of art, they still may contain different nuances of meaning for different persons. If we use elaborate definitions we can become so bogged down in detail as to lose all track of where we are going. And, if we use mathematical rules, we lose ground in the effort to be fair. [...] But we may reasonably conclude that at least a significant minority of indeterminate cases are likely to arise in a tax system that eschews comprehensive arbitrariness.[338]

In addition, in the African context, some countries have several national languages, and some have chosen to decide cases in vernacular languages. For example, South Africa has 11 official languages, each equal before the law, and legislation must be published in all these languages. This adds to the complexities. What will make sense to local populations in a traditional African language, if tax is an alien concept and fiscal literacy not widespread? In Rwanda until 2016, court cases were being decided in Kinyarwanda, the local language, making it impossible for other East African countries to refer to those cases as precedent. Since 2016, however, decisions are in English.[339]

5.5.4. Role of judicial interpretation
Miller explains:

> Whatever approach we choose towards the drafting of rules, the final arbiters of their meanings are the judges. Any discussion of the role of judges in the indeterminacy debate tends to mingle concepts of practical indeterminacy and theoretical indeterminacy. The law may be practically indeterminate because the judge fails to understand it, or to apply it correctly, or because the judge misunderstands or deliberately distorts the facts. The law may be theoretically indeterminate because it supports more than a single outcome and the judge must choose between right outcomes.[340]

In the interpretation of tax laws in Kenya, when a dispute arrives, the courts seem to favour a strict approach. In **Republic v Kenya Revenue Authority Exparte Bata Shoe Company (Kenya) Limited,**[341] the court stressed that in the interpretation of tax laws,

---

[338] Miller (1993) p. 44
[339] Waris (2014c)
[340] Miller (1993) p. 44
[341] [2014] eKLR

the plain language of Parliament should be adhered to lest the goods and services which Parliament did not want to tax are taxed as a consequence of the tax collector's misinterpretation of the laws. To achieve this purpose, the court was of the opinion that tax statutes must be strictly interpreted. The role of the court, it is said, is to discover the true intention of the rule maker when construing a taxing statute. Towards this end (citing a case from Malaysia which cited Lord Donovan in **Mangin v Inland Revenue Commissioner**[342]), the court is under a duty to:

> adopt an approach that produces neither injustice nor absurdity: in other words, an approach that promotes the purpose or object underlying the particular statute albeit that such purpose or object is not expressly set out therein.[343]

Kenyan courts have granted prohibition orders or quashed decisions of taxing authorities where the decision to tax has been improperly reached. In **Republic v Commissioner of Domestic Taxes (Large Taxpayers Office) Ex parte Barclays Bank of Kenya Limited,**[344] the court granted prohibition orders and quashed the decision of the Commissioner of Domestic Taxes on the basis of the manner in which they reached their decision, which did not meet the clarity required in taxation, but failed to take a step forward in neglected to explain what amounted to clarity in taxation.

In the 2005 **Unilever** case,[345] the result of indeterminacy in the law resulted in the Judge deciding to implement the OECD guiding principles on transfer pricing, which are recommendations, even though Kenya was not a member state of the OECD and even though all OECD states do not implement these recommendations.[346] Because Kenya is a member of the East African Community, this case has precedent value for the entire region.

---

[342] [1971] AC 739 (PC)
[343] Republic v Kenya Revenue Authority Exparte Bata Shoe Company (Kenya) Limited [2014] eKLR
[344] [2015] eKLR
[345] Unilever Kenya Limited v The Commissioner General, Kenya Revenue Authority [2005] eKLR
[346] Waris (2015)

In South Africa, the constitution seems to support a purposive approach[347] to the interpretation of fiscal legislation, however, in practice, courts still seem to favour the strict/literal approach. Cases such as **CIR v Simpson** are illustrative of the literal approach,[348] and cases such as **Savage v CIR** find issue with this approach and support a purposive one.[349]

5.6. Principles and rules

The cause of the extreme complexity of the tax system is that we have abandoned principles in favour of rules. John Avery Jones asked a very useful question:

> Could our tax legislation be rewritten so that it would be construed in accordance with principles rather than containing nothing but rules trying unsuccessfully to cover every eventuality?[350]

And he elaborated:

> Dworkin makes the distinction [...] between rules and principles.[351] The distinction is that rules are applicable in an all-or-nothing fashion, whereas principles are not. Principles can have exceptions, can conflict with one another; can, for example, apply only when conduct is reasonable; and they can give one guidance about how to deal with the points not expressly covered by the law. Rules do not conflict with each other (if they do, one of them must give and become a subsidiary rule). Principles do not conflict with rules. If a rule is clear, the rule applies and that is the end of it, even though it is an exception to the principle and therefore in conflict with it, [sic] But the real use for the principle is to determine what the rule means in the first place (and hopefully to reduce the amount of detail required in stating the rule), in which case there is no conflict.[352]

The question that arises in this section is whether tax legislation could be successfully rewritten in accordance with principles only

---

[347] "The purposive approach to statutory interpretation seeks to look for the purpose of the legislation before interpreting the words." http://e-lawresources.co.uk/Purposive-approach.php

[348] [1949] (4) SA 678 (A)

[349] [1951] 18 SATC 1

[350] Jones (1996) pp. 75-76 and Jones (1998) p. 263

[351] Dworkin (1977) at p. 22

[352] Jones (1996) pp. 75-76 and Jones (1998) p. 263

rather than rules. Either way, John Avery Jones argues that a set of principles needs to guide the interpretation of rules. This debate of rules vs. principles is reminiscent of debates between the application of civil and common law. Civil law, often practiced in France and francophone countries, tends to use a more rules-based approach, and common law, practiced in the UK and anglophone countries, takes on a more principle-based approach. Most common law countries in Africa use principles as set out in their constitution and in line with John Avery Jones thinking. This may be a solution to indeterminacy, by giving preference to fairness.

In the Tanzanian constitution,[353] a chapter is dedicated to the financing of the state. Article 138 states that:

> No tax of any kind shall be imposed save in accordance with a law enacted by Parliament or pursuant to a procedure lawfully prescribed and having the force of law by virtue of a law enacted by Parliament (author's translation).

Each year, the President has to direct persons to estimate revenue and expenditure and send the estimates to the National Assembly for approval, as set out in article 137. The tax legislation is laid down in 14 fundamental tax acts and several regulations.

In Guinea the institutions and legal procedures of the state are well developed. Its form of government is thus that of a tax state (see model in Appendix B). The budget process, for example, starts with the proposal of the finance act of the government to the National Assembly. The National Assembly then votes the budget. The court of audit oversees the implementation of the finance act. The President has limited power in the legal procedure. The President can ask the National Assembly for an additional deliberation. If the President does so, the finance act needs to be voted with a two-thirds majority.[354] Further, the finance act can be brought before the constitutional court by the President, one tenth of deputies, or the independent national institute for human rights for control of conformity with the constitution.[355] This protection by not only the

---

[353] Republic of Tanzania (2013)
[354] Republic of Guinea (2010) articles 75 and 79
[355] Republic of Guinea (2010) article 80

President but also other stakeholders limits the power of the President in the legislation.

Regarding the fiscal procedure, the revenue authority has a right of communication. The judicial authority can investigate a presumption of tax evasion, or any manoeuvre having the object or effect of fraud or of impairing a tax, whether civil, criminal or correctional in nature, even when terminated by a non-suit. The revenue authority also has a right of verification.

5.6.1. Principles-based legislation

Principles can be broad and will apply in all situations. By contrast, rules must be continuously crafted as more and more situations arise – or are contrived – that go far beyond the minds of drafts-people, Ministers or Parliament. The argument against legislation based on principles is that it is uncertain. The fact that this argument is paraded with a mantra does not mean that it is right. The argument is based on the fallacy that principles legislation is merely less detailed rules legislation, rather than legislation that is interpreted by reference to principles and explanatory memoranda in which the intentions of the legislature are expressed.

Lovric argues for principle-based drafting in the Australian context. In explaining what would make a draft principle-based, Lovric provides two criteria: the draft either has a broad or operative principle.[356] A broad principle is one which is flexible and oftentimes covers a wide range of factors at a "high level of abstraction." An operative principle, on the other hand, derives from duties, powers, rights and privileges.[357] He also describes the two basic and commonly used styles in principle-based drafting: top-down drafting and ground-up drafting. The former involves the use of an overarching principle and then building up and filling in with applications and details; the latter usually begins with rules, leaving it open for the rule maker to suggest a principle-based approach. This is also known as inductive drafting.

---

[356] Lovric (2010)
[357] Lovric (2010)

Lovric states that the uncertainty of principles-based legislation can be cured by having extra provisions providing clarifications, add-ons and carve-outs.[358] According to him, well-designed clarifications can yield more certainty and clarity as opposed to black letter rules. However, using Kenya's example, the 2018 Income Tax Bill[359] went through the normal pre-2010 constitutional process of a top-down approach, and the result shows clearly that the document does not reflect the 2010 constitution and the principles it delineates.

5.6.1.1. Control

One critical factor in principles-based legislation is the way the flesh put on the legislation is reviewed. Principles-based legislation is dependent on setting up a Parliamentary Committee, which hears evidence and can amend, as well as throw out, secondary legislation. It is this feature which contributes to fear of rules madness, which could complexify the system. Control could also be effected by courts rather than Parliament. This requires a widening of the appeals system to make the review of revenue decisions more accessible. This could be achieved by setting up a system of Special Commissioners or a Tax Ombudsman with the power to review the exercise of discretionary authority, as is being set up in many Latin American countries.[360]

Revenue decision-making is subject to a wide range of review from a wide variety of parliamentary, juridical and administrative bodies. In addition, in countries like Kenya, South Africa, Tunisia, and Zimbabwe, there is constitutionally mandated public participation. Open government procedures ensure that government activities, documents, and proceedings are available for inspection and therefore review through one of the many existing channels. Several African countries, like Kenya, are part of the UN Open Government Data project[361], and while a lot of data is available online, it is still hard to access tax and fiscal data. This area remains fairly opaque.

---

[358] Lovric (2010)
[359] Republic of Kenya (2018)
[360] IMF (2013) pp. 39-40
[361] https://publicadministration.un.org/en/ogd

Lovric[362] notes that the drafting of principles-based legislation can be demanding. Drafters must keep in mind the time required and the expertise required both in policy and in drafting. He points out that the principle-based approach should not be imposed on any type of regulation, even though it can be an optimal approach in many cases. Freedman[363] also notes that principles-based legislation requires great effort from all players, including rule-makers, revenue authorities, and even the taxpayer. Every effort should be made not to succumb to the temptation of trying to obtain a level of elaboration that would turn it into a mass of detailed provisions, as is the case in the UK.

The 2010 constitution of Kenya, at article 210, sets out the philosophy of the people.[364] In a context in which the capacity of the Kenyan people to understand legislation and legal processes has grown, the articulation of the philosophy of the people guides the development and implementation of a national value system and a Kenyan understanding of principles.[365] There is no doubt that a statement of principles at the beginning of a series of rules can help in the interpretation of the rules, which is something all countries, including African countries, should consider to help guide their lawmakers, enforcers and interpreters of laws, and other users of legislation.

5.6.1.2. Explanatory memoranda

Explanatory memoranda should be made available to explain each clause of any Finance Bill, going well beyond the existing published notes on clauses. The explanatory memoranda should include background information, the purpose of the clause, how it will operate, and other details such as examples to help users understand and interpret the legislation.

How is explanatory material used? First, it should rationalise a haphazard position, such as the one the House of Lords got itself

---

[362] Lovric (2010)
[363] Freedman (2010)
[364] Republic of Kenya (2010)
[365] Waris (2017a)

into in the landmark case of **Pepper v Hart**.[366] Under the new approach set out, courts can use ministerial statements in Parliament as a tiebreaker in cases where the statute is ambiguous. Having a comprehensive set of explanatory memoranda (expanded in the light of accepted amendments) ensures there is a full set of explanations, approved by Ministers before the Bill is debated and which afterwards Parliament could reasonably be assumed to have accepted.

Second, explanatory memoranda provide material on which a taxpayer may rely (and, if neglected, professional advisers could be sued). It is guidance that binds the state but not the taxpayer. For example, if the taxpayer and their advisers could show that the statutory words which Parliament used in establishing rules to express its will unambiguously, and regardless of any principles, were contradictory to its intention as expressed in the memorandum, then the words would prevail; form would triumph over substance and literalism over common sense. Along with the high-level principles, the explanatory memoranda are the means by which legislation is interpreted and provide certainty. It is by this means that the will of the society prevails: when the courts ask what it was that the people through the principles in the constitution intended, there is a comprehensive explanation at hand.

Tax policymakers have come to understand more thoroughly the principles of economics as they apply to income taxation (the time value of money[367] being a prominent example). They have also come to understand the ways in which business and investment can be structured to avoid income tax laws that are rudimentary in form. Policymakers have responded by urging parliaments rules that, while increasingly complex, have had the merit of immensely strengthening the income tax base and promoting horizontal equity by closing off planning opportunities available to some taxpayers but not to others.[368] Use of principles-based legislation, supported by

---

[366] Pepper (Inspector of Taxes) v Hart [1992] UKHL and AC 593 and STC 898
[367] "The time value of money (TVM) is the concept that money available at the present time is worth more than the identical sum in the future due to its potential earning capacity."
www.investopedia.com/terms/t/timevalueofmoney.asp
[368] Prebble (1998)

explanatory memoranda, help ensures that fiscal laws maintain their underpinnings of fairness and justice at all times.

5.6.1.3. *Conflicting principles and conflicting rules*

Theoretically, cases where two principles conflict are easier to resolve than cases where two rules conflict, because conflicting principles can exist side by side, but if rules conflict the court must decide which takes precedence.[369] However, tax law does not lend itself to the resolution of conflict between principles any more than it lends itself to the resolution of conflict between rules. Somewhat unusually, the principle about bad debts allows taxpayers themselves to decide when this kind of loss will be considered for tax purposes. It is hard to see how a court could make a logical choice about that principle.

5.6.1.4. *What role is there for principles?*

One of the advantages of principle-based drafting of tax legislation is that it makes it easier for the taxpayer to understand the legislation. It may also avoid loopholes in the law and make the implementation of complex regulatory systems simpler.[370]

John Avery Jones advocates a two-level solution. At the top are more abstract principles, such as those in the 1992 Treaty on European Union and the 2010 Kenyan constitution. Then there are more specific principles, such as found in the preamble to European Union legislation. The second level is the legislation itself, which is interpreted with the aid of the higher-level principles as well as the explanatory memoranda. There is no third level of detailed legislation, but, of course, below the legislation is revenue practice, which is now published.[371]

A possible solution for the resolution of conflicts is to refer to a higher principle, stated in terms of greater abstraction. One would then need examples to be persuaded. This begs the question of whether income tax law has such higher principles that can be stated

---

[369] Shapiro (2007) p. 9
[370] Lovric (2010)
[371] Jones (1996)

in terms sufficiently specific to be useful in instances of conflict. The answer is probably no. Income tax law is a compromise between on the one hand a desire to assess gains across a neutral, comprehensive tax base, and on the other hand all sorts of political and administrative forces. These forces at play include the need to nominate a geographical source for income, the need to divide income into portions delimited by time, the difficulty of valuing and taxing benefits that taxpayers enjoy from their own labour or assets, the emotional and political reaction to capital gains taxes in some jurisdictions, and so on.

Freedman[372] states in the longstanding debate on the use of principles-based legislation, as suggested by John Avery Jones, that using the approach will not provide a solution to all ills. While admitting that the approach has not been entirely successful, especially in Australia, she cautions that the experiment should not be abandoned. According to Freedman, using principles as a drafting tool should help in focusing legislators on the absence of clear underlying policy in instances where that is the problem.

5.6.2. Rules-based legislation

Rules-based legislation involves elaborate tax rules that are long, detailed, specific, and interconnected. It is based on the argument that the rules need clarity and must be as determinate as possible. D'Amato[373], Greenawalt[374], Kress[375], and Schauer[376] have all debated the issue of legal indeterminacy in the context of tax law. D'Amato asserts that law is entirely indeterminate.[377] Greenawalt believes that "many legal questions have determinate answers."[378] Kress believes

---

[372] Freedman (2010)

[373] D'Amato (1989, 1990)

[374] Greenawalt (1990, 1992)

[375] Kress (1989)

[376] Schauer (1991)

[377] D'Amato (1989) p. 170

[378] Many legal questions have determinate answers that (1) would be arrived at unopposed by legal experts and (2) are unopposed by powerful arguments.

that "the indeterminacy of the law is no more than moderate."[379] Schauer argues that highly determinate rule systems are possible.[380]

The debate over law's determinacy has been characterized as the central issue in modern legal scholarship.[381] Whether or not this is so, this debate sheds light on the relationship between rules and fairness. The indeterminacy debate demonstrates that, in an important sense, the proper role of rules in our tax systems is a question of philosophy rather than of tax theory. The vast proliferation of rules in tax law is defended by the belief that elaborate rules can render tax law both fair and certain. The unspoken assumptions are that rules determine outcomes in a mechanical fashion and that such a process can produce fairness. The indeterminacy debate offers insights about how rules work, which insights may cause us to rethink views about the value of elaborate rules to achieve fairness.

Malcolm James is of the opinion that uncertainty is inherent in both rule-based and principle-based methods of drafting tax legislation. Uncertainty is more apparent in principles-based legislation, because principles only provide guidance which must be applied to specific situations. However, while rules may appear prescriptive, uncertainty also arises in rules-based legislation, because the interpretation of legislation is a matter of the interpretation of words, and uncertainty is a result of instances when their meaning in context is ambiguous. A shift from rules-based to principles-based legislation, according to James, has the potential to shift power from the taxpayer to the state.[382]

The reason for this, according to James,[383] is that it would be more difficult for the taxpayer to challenge decisions made on the grounds that a scheme was, for example, deemed to be abusive or artificial, because the lack of clear criteria in interpreting these terms means that it is more difficult to rule that the interpretation by tax officials or the lower court was wrong or unreasonable. Both rule-based and principle-based approaches have their pros and cons, and

---

[379] Kress (1989) p. 283
[380] Schauer (1991) pp. 220-38
[381] D'Amato (1989) p. 148 and D'Amato (2010)
[382] James (2010)
[383] James (2010)

James concludes that neither can be relied upon for objective and value-free decision-making systems. Instead, societal perceptions of objectivity may enhance the legitimacy of decision-making systems, effectively limiting the operation of discretionary power. James goes on to explain how the theories of power as presented by Lukes[384] offer a useful lens through which to observe the operation especially of judicial power.

5.7. Conclusion

Laws must be fair and just, and the determinacy of laws adds to their legitimacy. If one were to argue for fiscal legitimacy through the deepening of the relationship between the state and society, then, most likely, a principle-based approach to tax legislation is more suitable than a rule-based approach. The scholars cited and referenced in this chapter referred to developed country contexts with well-equipped and well-trained technocrats and judges. In developing country contexts, like many in Africa, administrations can be weak and capacity low. As a result, the need to stick to a more principle-based approach reflective of the society cannot be emphasized enough, in order to ensure the growth of the fiscal legitimacy of the state and the continent. This becomes even more important with the coming into force of the African Continental Free Trade Agreement.

In addition, in the use of explanatory memoranda, guidance is crucial, especially because the judiciary remains weak. There should be allowances for reliance on expert witnesses and on more information from lawmakers. This should include reference to the guiding principles for the society as articulated in the constitution and to legislative drafters for clearer understandings of their intentions in legislative explanations. However, once one moves beyond the spirit of law, one must also be guided by the economic system in place in a country. Different countries globally have different types of economies and economic systems, which are in turn guided by principles.

---

[384] Lukes (2005)

Chapter 6

Recommendations

Rain does not fall on one roof alone.

Proverb from Cameroon and Congo

6.1. Domestic and regional level recommendations

6.1.1. Developing compliant taxpayers

A government, through the ministry of education, should issue a guide to help citizens and residents understand not only taxes but the entire fiscal system. This guide should explain to the layperson, the following: the reason for taxes; other sources of revenue; how taxes are levied; what taxes are levied; the participative budget process; how the entire budget is spent; and where and how national budget information can be accessed. This learning should also be part of the education system of the country from primary school level.

All citizens and residents should have either a national registration number or a tax number that is issued simultaneously upon receipt of their national identity card at the age of 18.

Information on the fiscal system of the state should be easily accessible across the continent and in languages that citizens understand.

6.1.2. Supporting facilitators of fiscal processes

For clear guidance, lawyers and judges, should carefully consider the following:

a.   The oath of allegiance and the code of professional ethics clearly set out that Advocates are officers of the court; this requires reinforcement and reminders to Advocates and others;

b.   Advocates must be active in ensuring that legislation guiding them is passed without bias;

c.   The role of the Advocate as advisor must necessarily preclude advice on money laundering and illicit financial flows, which practices affect state security;

d. The Law Society should circulate a practice note or lawyers guide, inspired by documents of the International Bar Association but domesticated, for all practicing Advocates on what advice can and cannot be given and what would form a breach of ethics;

e. Advocates ought to be clearly guided on (1) their obligation to identify their clients, (2) what a suspicious transaction looks like and their obligation to report it, (3) what amounts to proceeds of crime, and (4) their obligation not to conceal or disguise the proceeds of crimes; and

f. Due to the lack of fiscal related training, when there is a problem with the revenue authority and an assessment is needed, it goes to the judiciary, however, African judges have limited understandings of fiscal law, which situation should be rectified.

6.1.3. Updating treaties, laws and policies

Treaties, laws and policies must be updated to reflect national, regional and continental interests, as described below, and good practices put in place in relation to how firms operate in national and regional spaces on the continent.

a. Conduct **media literacy** to ensure journalists and populations are aware of and have knowledge about corporate practices;

b. Consider a **company as a unitary entity** and allow states to deal with its activities globally, in conjunction with monitoring by the UN Tax Committee;

c. Develop **name-and-shame lists** of organisations and professionals to be banned from certain bodies or from work in certain areas;

d. Control **access to markets and loans**, including by MNEs and other firms;

e. Apply **doctrines of command responsibility**, with inspiration from how international criminal law prohibits and punishes criminal activity;

f. There is also a role for domestic courts which could also be developed within regional and international bodies. Nationalise domestic assets or confiscate them and **ban offending corporations** from operating in the country or region for a period that is punitive, e.g. 30 or 50 years, and would affect the sourcing of raw materials and/or market access;

g. **Cross-reference countries' losses in taxes, human rights indicators, and progress towards SDGs** to understand and demonstrate interrelations between taxation, human rights, and development and compare to international benchmarks and exemplary countries; and

h. Add terms in tax treaties, including bilateral investment treaties (BITs) and agreements (BIAs) and double tax agreement (DTAs), to **justify the collection of resources and consequences for noncompliance** as well as specify responsibilities and requirements for company registry and online access to company documents.

6.2. Continental level recommendations

Set up a multidisciplinary fiscal team of experts to elaborate policy guidelines and support policy development at subnational, national, regional and continental levels, allowing for input from the continent and influence of interactions with the rest of the world.

Chapter 7

Conclusion

Kulipa Ushuru ni Kujitegemea.
Paying taxes is being independent.

Kenya Revenue Authority

Understanding a country's fiscal system requires unpacking the system. It must be mapped out, with its constituent parts, and reflected upon. Does it follow a rhythm, line of thinking or vision? Value must be added when putting it back together, and reflection on it must continue. Based on available information, this book has mapped out the direction the continent is taking. Several challenges should and can be addressed and resolved.

There is a disconnect between constitutions, legislation, regulations, and policy. There is lack of access to adequate information about many of the national endeavours that should be supporting law and policy. In many instances on the continent, policy directions are not translating well in regional, national and subnational spaces.

All government revenue including tax must be generated, but for specific expenditures. Two rules should guide the process. First, the cost of application and administration must not exceed 1% of the total revenues collected. Second, estimated revenues must be tallied with actual revenues. These practices are often compromised in the fiscal and political processes leading up to tax decisions at domestic levels. Ibn Khaldun argued that justice is the underlying bedrock which cannot be compromised, and Adam Smith simply considered it a pillar or canon which *could* be compromised. A good tax system that is fiscally legitimate ought never compromise on the principle of justice as espoused by Ibn Khaldun.

Considering a tax system in isolation from other items of public revenue or expenditure is an incomplete and unrealistic exercise. Taxation is only one part of the total budget of the government, which is why this book discussed the entirety of the fiscal system.

A tax system has many dimensions, including volume, composition, rates, coverage, timings of collection and modes of collection. It is nearly impossible to choose theoretically the best system. Government will generally settle for a compromise between conflicting considerations and, therefore, in the end, settles for a suboptimum tax system.

Normally, each taxpayer desires to be freed from the burden of tax and does not mind it if it is borne by others. It is essential that a good tax system be equitable to all taxpayers. Attitudes towards taxes are also influenced by factors such as the political climate, natural calamities, and the economic situation. Changes in the tax system can be brought about slowly and in stages. A sudden disruption is never successful.

Any country should have teams of experts from a cross-section of the stakeholders in society to help develop its fiscal laws and policies, based on its objectives. There are several layers to this. First, there is the complementary role of municipal and national taxes. Second, there are liaisons with the international community in applying tax laws. Third, bilateral agreements with other nations, for example double taxation avoidance agreements, must be considered. Fourth, planning and foresight are necessary. National plans are used to warn citizens of impending tax burdens. Fifth, in the budget speech, government indicates the nature of the tax in question, its administrative machinery, the rates, and the tax threshold. Unfortunately, to date, few countries on the continent have released a clear tax policy, guideline or set of objectives.

There is no perfect fiscal system, only the suboptimal, but as the Kossi say, "If the rhythm of the drumbeat changes, the dance step must adapt."

References

Action Aid. 2015. *The West African giveaway: Use and abuse of corporate tax incentives in ECOWAS.* Johannesburg: Action Aid. www.globaltaxjustice.org/sites/default/files/the_west_african_giveaway_2.pdf

African Development Bank. 2018a. *African economic outlook.* Abidjan: African Development Bank.

African Development Bank. 2018b. *African statistical yearbook.* Abidjan: African Development Bank.

African Union. 2013. *Agenda 2063: The Africa we want.* https://au.int/en/Agenda2063/popular_version

African Union Department of Economic Affairs, Waris A. and Magara W. 2019. Dataset mapping 2018 African Union trade statistics. www.cfs.uonbi.ac.ke

African Union and UNECA. 2015. *Report of the high level panel on illicit financial flows from Africa.* Addis Ababa. http://repository.uneca.org/handle/10855/22695

Ahmad J., Devarajan S., Khemani, S. and Shah S. 2005. "Decentralization and service delivery." Policy research working paper 3603. World Bank, Washington, DC. https://openknowledge.worldbank.org/handle/10986/8933

Ajayi S. I. 1991. "Macroeconomic approach to external debt: The case of Nigeria." AERC research paper 8. African Economic Research Consortium, Nairobi. www.africaportal.org/publications/macroeconomic-approach-to-external-debt-the-case-of-nigeria

Akech J. M. M. 2006. "Development partners and governance of public procurement in Kenya: Enhancing democracy in the administration of aid." Working paper 2006/3, Global Administrative Law Series, NYU Institute for International Law and Justice (IILJ). http://iilj.org/wp-content/uploads/2016/08/Akech-Development-Partners-and-Governance-of-Public-Procurement-in-Kenya-2006-2.pdf

Akinkugbe O., Chama-Chiliba C. M. and Tlotlego N. 2012. "Health financing and catastrophic payments for health care: evidence from household-level survey data in Botswana and Lesotho."

African Development Review 24(4): 358-370. https://doi.org/10.1111/1467-8268.12006

Alt J. 2019. "Catholic social teaching and taxation: Guidelines towards a socially more just and ecologically more sustainable world." *Journal on Financing for Development* 1(1): 47-69. http://uonjournals.uonbi.ac.ke/ojs/index.php/ffd/issue/view/54

Armed conflict location and event data project. 2014. *Guide to dataset use for humanitarian and development practitioners.* ACLED. www.acleddata.com/wp-content/uploads/2014/01/ACLED_Guide-to-Dataset-Use-for-Humanitarian-and-Development-Practitioners_2014.pdf

Arnason R. 2008. "Natural resource rents: Theoretical clarification." Working paper WP08:07. Institute of Economic Studies.

ATAF, Waris A. and Magara W. 2019. Dataset mapping taxpayer data with 2017 population statistics. www.uonbi.ac.ke

Bajpai P. 2019. "How central banks control the supply of money." Investopedia. Accessed 19 July 2019. www.investopedia.com/articles/investing/053115/how-central-banks-control-supply-money.asp

Beegle K., Christiaensen L., Dabalen A. and Gaddis I. 2016. *Poverty in a rising Africa: Africa poverty report.* Washington, DC.: World Bank. www.worldbank.org/en/region/afr/publication/poverty-rising-africa-poverty-report

Bhatia H. L. 2018. *Public finance* (29th ed). New Delhi: Vikas.

Bird R. M. and Zolt E. M. 2003. "Introduction to tax policy design and development." Prepared for a course on practical issues of tax policy in developing countries. World Bank, Washington, DC. https://gsdrc.org/document-library/introduction-to-tax-policy-design-and-development

Blank J. D. and Osofsky L. 2017. "Simplexity: Plain language and the tax law." *Emory Law Journal* 66(2): 189-264. http://law.emory.edu/elj/content/volume-66/issue-2/articles/simplexity-plain-language-tax.html

Blum W. J. 1976. "Contemporary canons of taxation." *Taxes: The Tax Magazine* 54(5): 277-279. See first page at

https://heinonline.org/HOL/Page?handle=hein.journals/taxt
m54&div=53&g_sent=1&casa_token=&collection=journals

Bogenschneider B. 2016. "Factual indeterminacy in international tax law." *BRICS Law Journal* 3(3): 73-102. https://doi.org/10.21684/2412-2343-2016-3-3-73-102

Brennan G. and Buchanan J. M. 1980. *The power to tax: Analytical foundations of a fiscal constitution.* New York: Cambridge University Press.

Brosio G. and Outreville, J. F. 2011. "Maintaining taxes at the centre despite decentralisation: Interactions with national reforms." Working paper no. 10/2011. International Centre for Economic Research.
www.bemservizi.unito.it/repec/icr/wp2011/ICERwp10-11.pdf

Burg D. F. 2004. *A world history of tax rebellions: An encyclopedia of tax rebels, revolts, and riots from antiquity to the present.* New York: Routledge.

Buttner T. 1970. "The economic and social character of pre-colonial states in tropical Africa." *Journal of the Historical Society of Nigeria* 5(2): 275-289. Read here with Jstor login and password:
www.jstor.org/stable/pdf/41856846.pdf?refreqid=excelsior%3
A95d9382fa290672d75a97c6138473914

Cadesky M., Hayes I. and Russell D. 2016. *Towards greater fairness in taxation: A model taxpayer charter.* Amsterdam: IBFD.
www.ibfd.org/IBFD-Products/Towards-Greater-Fairness-
Taxation-Model-Taxpayer-Charter

CIA. 2017a. "The world factbook - country comparison - military expenditures." Accessed 15 May 2017.
https://www.cia.gov/library/publications/the-world-
factbook/rankorder/2034rank.html#tz

CIA. 2017b. "The world factbook - Tanzania." Accessed 15 May 2017. https://www.cia.gov/library/publications/the-world-
factbook/geos/tz.html

Collier P. 2006. "Africa's economic growth: Opportunities and constraints." Paper prepared for the African Development Bank.
www.afdb.org/fileadmin/uploads/afdb/Documents/Knowledg
e/09484307-EN-AFRICA-S-ECONOMIC-GROWTH-
OPPORTUNITIES-AND-CONSTRAINTS.PDF

Cornell D. L. 1988. "Institutionalization of meaning, recollective imagination and the potential for transformative legal interpretation." *University of Pennsylvania Law Review* 136(4): 1135-1229. https://scholarship.law.upenn.edu/cgi/viewcontent.cgi?article=3908&context=penn_law_review

Crawford G. and Hartmann C. (Eds.). 2008. *Decentralisation in Africa: A pathway out of poverty and conflict?* Amsterdam: Amsterdam University Press.

Curtis A. and Todorova O. 2012. "Spotlight on Africa's transfer pricing landscape." PricewaterhouseCoopers, London. Accessed 2 November 2018. www.pwc.com/gx/en/tax/transfer-pricing/management-strategy/assets/pwc-transfer-pricing-africa-pdf.pdf

Dalton H. 2009. *Principles of public finance.* London: Routledge. First published in 1922. www.worldcat.org/title/principles-of-public-finance/oclc/540798566/viewport

D'Amato A. A. 1989. *How to understand the law.* Dobbs Ferry: Transnational Juris.

D'Amato A. A. 1990. "Pragmatic indeterminacy." *Northwestern University Law Review* 85: 148-189. https://scholarlycommons.law.northwestern.edu/cgi/viewcontent.cgi?article=1077&context=facultyworkingpapers

Deloitte. 2015. "International tax: Namibia highlights." Accessed 30 July 2019. https://www2.deloitte.com/content/dam/Deloitte/global/Documents/Tax/dttl-tax-namibiahighlights-2015.pdf

Deloitte. 2017. "Namibia budget 2017/18 commentary: Making impact where it matters." Accessed 30 July 2019. www2.deloitte.com/na/en/pages/tax/articles/namibia-budget-2017-2018.html#

Diallo A. L. 2017. "Autopsie d'une révolte populaire à Boké : les problèmes d'eau et du courant électrique." Accessed 29 July 2019. http://guineematin.com/actualites/autopsie-dune-revolte-populaire-a-boke-les-problemes-deau-et-du-courant-electrique

Dworkin R. 1977. *Taking rights seriously*. Cambridge: Harvard University Press.

Easterly W. and Rebelo S. 1993. "Fiscal policy and economic growth: An empirical investigation." *Journal of Monetary Economics* 32(3): 417-458. https://doi.org/10.1016/0304-3932(93)90025-B

Elmi N. 2019. "The colonial aftermath in digitalising tax." *Journal on Financing for Development* 1(1): 80-96. http://uonjournals.uonbi.ac.ke/ojs/index.php/ffd/issue/view/54

Endicott T. A. O. 1996. "Linguistic indeterminacy." *Oxford Journal of Legal Studies* 16(4): 667-697. https://doi.org/10.1093/ojls/16.4.667

Ernst and Young. 2015. "Overview of government procurement procedures in sub-Saharan Africa: Angola, Botswana, Namibia and South Africa." Accessed 2 November 2018. https://assets.publishing.service.gov.uk/government/uploads/system/uploads/attachment_data/file/431557/Overview_of_government_procurement_procedures_in_sub-Saharan_Africa.pdf

Ernst and Young. 2017. "Namibia budget proposals." Accessed 29 July 2019. www.ey.com

Eurodad. 2006. "World Bank and IMF conditionality: A development injustice." Accessed 24 July 2019. www.eurodad.org/files/pdf/454-world-bank-and-imf-conditionality-a-development-injustice.pdf

*Eustice J. S. 1989. "Tax complexity and the tax practitioner." *Tax Law Review* 45(22): 7-24.

Fabian Society. 2000. *Paying for progress: A new politics of tax for public spending*. London: Fabian Society, Commission on Taxation and Citizenship. https://books.google.co.uk/books/about/Paying_for_Progress.html?id=b9azAAAAIAAJ

Federal Republic of Nigeria. 2007. Federal inland revenue service (establishment) act. www.orandcconsultants.com/Downloads/FIRS_ESTABLISHMENT_ACT.pdf

Fox M. 2015, Mar 10. "Why we need a global wealth tax: Piketty." CNBC. Accessed 22 July 2019 www.cnbc.com/2015/03/10/why-we-need-a-global-wealth-tax-piketty.html

Frank J. 1930. *Law and the modern mind.* New York: Brentano's.

Freedman J. 2010. "Improving (not perfecting) tax legislation: Rules and principles revisited." *British Tax Review* 6: 717-739.

Fuller L. 1958. "Positivism and fidelity to law: A reply to Professor Hart." *Harvard Law Review* 71(4): 630-672.

Fuo O. 2015. "Public participation in decentralised governments in Africa: Making ambitious constitutional guarantees more responsive." *African Human Rights Law Journal* 15:167-191.

GAN Business Anti-Corruption Portal. 2018. "South Africa corruption report." Accessed 6 October 2019. www.business-anti-corruption.com/country-profiles/south-africa

Gichuki E. N. 2015. "Tax administration reforms in Kenya: Identifying lessons to model a strategy for sustainable administration of county taxes." PhD thesis, University of Nairobi School of Law, Kenya.

Greenawalt K. 1990. "How law can be determinate." *University of California Law Review* 38(1): 1-86.

Greenawalt K. 1992. *Law and objectivity.* Oxford: Oxford University Press.

GTZ/GIZ. No date. "Why care about taxation and gender equality?" Deutsche Gesellschaft für Technische Zusammenarbeit (GTZ), which, through a merger, became Deutsche Gesellschaft für Internationale Zusammenarbeit (GIZ) in 2011. Accessed 1 September 2019. www.oecd.org/dac/gender-development/44896295.pdf

Hart H. L. A. 1994. *The concept of law* (2nd ed.). New York: Oxford University Press.

Hasnain Z. 2008. "Devolution, accountability, and service delivery: Some insights from Pakistan." Policy research working paper no. 4610. World Bank South Asia Region Poverty Reduction Economic Management Department. http://unpan1.un.org/intradoc/groups/public/documents/apcity/unpan047337.pdf

Heald D. and McLeod A. 2010. "The taxation and borrowing powers of the UK devolved administrations." Conference paper presented to the Political Studies Association's specialist group conference on British and comparative territorial politics, University of Oxford, 7-8 January.

Ho K. M. and Turley C. 2018. "New boundaries of tax." In *What to tax: Perspectives on tax are changing; tax is changing perspectives* (pp. 20-25). KMPG International. Accessed 1 September 2019. https://assets.kpmg/content/dam/kpmg/xx/pdf/2018/10/what-to-tax-web.pdf

Hoffman M. and Rumsey M. 2012. *International and foreign legal research: A coursebook* (2nd ed.). Leiden: Martinus Nijhoff.

Horton M. and El-Ganainy A. 2018. "Fiscal policy: Taking and giving away." International Monetary Fund. Accessed 19 July 2019. www.imf.org/external/pubs/ft/fandd/basics/fiscpol.htm

Hume D. 1748. *An enquiry concerning human understanding.* Oxford: Oxford University Press

ICIJ. 2014. "Luxembourg leaks." Accessed 29 July 2019. www.icij.org/investigations/luxembourg-leaks/explore-documents-luxembourg-leaks-database

ICIJ. 2016. "Swiss leaks." Accessed 29 July 2019. https://projects.icij.org/swiss-leaks

ICIJ. 2017. "Paradise papers: Secrets of the global elite." Accessed 29 July 2019. www.icij.org/investigations/paradise-papers

ICIJ. 2018. "The Panama papers: Exposing the rogue offshore finance industry." Accessed 29 July 2019. www.icij.org/investigations/panama-papers

ICIJ. 2019. "Mauritius leaks." Accessed 30 July 2019. www.icij.org/investigations/mauritius-leaks/treasure-island-leak-reveals-how-mauritius-siphons-tax-from-poor-nations-to-benefit-elites

ICPAK. 2016. *Kenya revenue analysis 2010-2015: A historical perspective to revenue performance in Kenya.* Nairobi: Institute of Certified Public Accountants of Kenya.

IMF. 2013. "How can an excessive volume of tax disputes be dealt with?" International Monetary Fund. Accessed 20 August 2019. www.imf.org/external/np/leg/tlaw/2013/eng/tdisputes.pdf

IMF. 2014. *Government finance statistics manual.* Washington, DC: International Monetary Fund. www.imf.org/external/pubs/ft/gfs/manual/gfs.htm

IMF. 2017. "Senegal: Outstanding purchases and loans as of April 30, 2017." International Monetary Fund. Accessed 29 July 2019. www.imf.org/external/np/fin/tad/extcredt1.aspx?memberKey 1=840&date1key=2017-04-30&roption=Y

IMF. 2019a. "Regional capacity development centres." International Monetary Fund. Accessed 24 July 2019. www.imf.org/en/About/Factsheets/Sheets/2017/06/14/imf-regional-capacity-development-initiatives

IMF. 2019b. "Rwanda." Country report no. 19/211. International Monetary Fund, Washington, DC. Accessed 20 August 2019. www.imf.org/~/media/Files/Publications/CR/2019/1RWAE A2019001.ashx

IPS. 2017. "Droogte in Oost-Afrika drijft voedselprijzen de hoogte in." Accessed 15 May 2017. www.mo.be/nieuws/droogte-oost-afrika-drijft-voedselprijzen-de-hoogte

James M. 2010. "Humpty Dumpty's guide to tax law: Rules, principles and certainty in taxation." *Critical Perspectives on Accounting* 21(7): 573-583. https://doi.org/10.1016/j.cpa.2010.03.007

Jones J. A. 1996. "Tax law: Rules or principles?" *Fiscal Studies* 17(3): 63-89. www.ifs.org.uk/publications/2274 and https://doi.org/10.1111/j.1475-5890.1996.tb00494.x

Jones J. A. 1998. "Tax law: Rules or principles?" In M. Andenas and F. Jacobs (Eds.), *European community law in the English courts* (pp. 251-276) Oxford: Clarendon.

Khaldun I. 1377. *Muqaddimah* (translated by F. Rosenthal). Accessed 28 August 2019. https://asadullahali.files.wordpress.com/2012/10/ibn_khaldun -al_muqaddimah.pdf

Khamisi J. 2018. *Looters and grabbers: 54 years of corruption and plunder by the elite, 1963-2017.* Plano: Jodey. https://yeauganda.files.wordpress.com/2018/08/kenya-looters-and-grabbers-54-years-of-corruption-and-plunder-by-the-elite-1963-2017.pdf

162

Kingdom of Morocco. 2011. Constitution of Morocco. Accessed 2 November 2018. www.constituteproject.org/constitution/Morocco_2011.pdf

Kingdom of Morocco. 2019. Code général des impôts.

Kipngetich J. 2001. "Management of public finances." Accessed 20 August 2019. www.katibainstitute.org

Kiser E. and Sacks A. 2009. "Improving tax administration in contemporary African states: Lessons from history." In M. Martin, A. Mehrotra and M. Prasad (Eds.), *The new fiscal sociology: Taxation in comparative and historical perspective* (pp. 183-200). Cambridge: Cambridge University Press. https://doi.org/10.1017/CBO9780511627071.012

KPMG. 2016. "Senegal fiscal guide 2015/2016." Accessed 30 July 2019. https://assets.kpmg.com/content/dam/kpmg/pdf/2016/05/S enegal-Fiscal-Guide-2015-2016.pdf

Kress K. 1989. "Legal indeterminacy." *California Law Review* 77(2): 283-337. Accessed 20 August 2019. https://doi.org/10.15779/Z380B17

Kvamme F. 2017. "The challenge of taxation in African countries." Norwegian Institute of International Affairs. Accessed 30 July 2019. www.nupi.no/en/News/The-challenge-of-taxation-in-African-countries

Ladepeche diplomatique. 2013. "Autosuffisance alimentaire en Guinée : l'agriculture, un appui au développement rural." Accessed 23 August 2019. www.seneweb.com/news/Afrique/autosuffisance-alimentaire-en-guinee-l-rsquo-agriculture-   un-appui-au-developpement-rural_n_101712.html

Lerner A. P. 1959. *The economics of control: Principles of welfare economics.* New York: Macmillan.

Llewellyn K. N. 1960. *The bramble bush: On our law and its study.* New Orleans: Quid Pro.

Locke J. 1690. *Two treatises of government.* London: Printed for Awnsham Churchill. Accessed 30 July 2019. https://history.hanover.edu/courses/excerpts/eurloc.html

Lovric D. 2010. "Principles-based drafting: Experiences from tax drafting." *The Loophole*, Journal of the Commonwealth Association of Legislative Counsel, 19(3): 16-29. www.calc.ngo/sites/default/files/loophole/dec-2010.pdf

Lukes S. 2005. *Power: A radical view* (2nd ed.). London: Palgrave Macmillan. http://voidnetwork.gr/wp-content/uploads/2016/09/Power-A-Radical-View-Steven-Lukes.pdf

Malthus T. R. 1814. *Observations on the effects of the corn laws, and of a rise or fall in the price of corn on the agriculture and general wealth of the country.* London: J Johnson.

Martinez M. and Mlachila M. 2013. "The quality of the recent high-growth episode in sub-Saharan Africa." Working paper 13/53. International Monetary Fund, Washington, DC. www.imf.org/external/pubs/ft/wp/2013/wp1353.pdf

McCaffery E. J. 1990. "The holy grail of tax simplification." *Wisconsin Law Review* 5: 1267-1322.

McGee R. W. 2011. *The philosophy of taxation and public finance.* Boston: Kluwer Academic.

Mekonnen D. R. 2015. "Introductory note on the constitution of Eritrea." Accessed 29 July 2019 on web site of Institute for International and Comparative Law in Africa, University of Pretoria. www.icla.up.ac.za/images/country_reports/eritrea_country_report.pdf

Meltzer A. H. 2000. "The report of the international financial institution advisory commission: Comments on the critics." International Financial Institution Advisory Commission.

Mensah E. 2015. "Navigating Ghana's tax incentives regime: An impossible mission?" PowerPoint. Accessed 30 July 2019. www.un.org/esa/ffd/wp-content/uploads/2015/04/2015TIBP_CountryExperience-Ghana.pdf

Miller J. A. 1993. "Indeterminacy, complexity, and fairness: Justifying rule simplification in the law of taxation." *Washington Law Review* 68(1): 1-78. https://digitalcommons.law.uw.edu/wlr/vol68/iss1/2

Mirrlees J., Adam S., Besley T., Blundell R., Bond S., Chote R., ... and Poterba J. 2011. *Tax by design: The Mirrlees review* (1ˢᵗ ed.). Oxford: Oxford University Press.

Mlachila M., Tapsoba R. and Tapsoba S. J. A. 2014. "A quality of growth index for developing countries: A proposal." Working paper 14/172. International Monetary Fund, Washington, DC. www.imf.org/external/pubs/ft/wp/2014/wp14172.pdf

Mo Ibrahim Foundation. 2017. Ibrahim index of African governance. http://mo.ibrahim.foundation/iiag

Morabito V. and Barkoczy S. 1996. "What is a tax? The erosion of the 'Latham definition.'" *Revenue Law Journal* 1(6): 43-63.

Mourre G. and Reut A. 2019. "Non-tax revenue in the European Union: A source of fiscal risk?" *International Tax and Public Finance* 26(1): 198-223. https://doi.org/10.1007/s10797-018-9498-z

Moyi E. and Ronge E. 2006. "*Taxation and tax modernization in Kenya: A diagnosis of performance and options for further reform.*" Nairobi: Institute of Economic Affairs. www.researchgate.net/publication/265378561_Taxation_and_Tax_Modernization_in_Kenya_A_Diagnosis_of_Performance_and_Options_for_Further_Reform

Mumford A. (2002). *Taxing culture: Towards a theory of tax collection law.* Aldershot: Ashgate.

Musell R. M. 2009. *Understanding government budgets: A practical guide.* New York: Routledge.

Muthoni K. 2017. "Court blocks Shs 3.3 billion extra pay to Kenyan MPs." Standard Media. Accessed 10 February 2017. www.standardmedia.co.ke/article/2001228884/court-blocks-sh3-3-billion-extra-pay-to-kenyan-mps

Mwencha P. M. 2019. "Taxation of electronic commerce: A commentary." *Journal on Financing for Development* 1(1):70-79. http://uonjournals.uonbi.ac.ke/ojs/index.php/ffd/issue/view/54

Nantob N. 2014. "Taxes and economic growth in developing countries: A dynamic panel approach." Accessed 23 July 2019. https://mpra.ub.uni-muenchen.de/61346

Ng'wanakilala, F. 2017. "Tanzania sacks 9,900 civil servants over 'fake degrees.'" Reuters. Accessed 15 May 2017.

www.reuters.com/article/us-tanzania-corruption-idUSKBN17U24T

Nsehe, M. 2015, Dec 1. "Corruption and 'tenderpreneurs' bring Kenya's economy to its knees." Forbes. Accessed 24 August 2019. www.forbes.com/sites/mfonobongnsehe/2015/12/01/corrupt ion-and-tenderpreneurs-bring-kenyas-economy-to-its-knees

Odhiambo F. T. 2011, Jul 14. "Demystifying stamp duty charges." Standard Media. Accessed 31 August 2019. www.standardmedia.co.ke/article/2000038869/demystifying-stamp-duty-charges

Odhiambo O. and Olushola O. 2018. "Taxation and economic growth in a resource-rich country: The case of Nigeria." In J. Iwin-Garzyńska (Ed.), *Taxes and Taxation Trends* (pp. 61-81). London: IntechOpen. http://dx.doi.org/10.5772/66617

OECD. 1996. "Definition of taxes." Document DAFFE/MAI/EG2(96)3 by expert group no. 3 on treatment of tax issues in the multilateral agreement on investment (MAI). OECD, Paris. www1.oecd.org/daf/mai/pdf/eg2/eg2963e.pdf

OECD. 2008. "Tax administration in OECD and selected non-OECD countries: Comparative information series." OECD, Paris. www.oecd.org/tax/forum-on-tax-administration/publications-and-products/comparative

OECD. 2014. *Part 1 of a report to G20 development working group on the impact of [base erosion and profit shifting] BEPS in low income countries.* Paris: OECD. Accessed 15 May 2017. www.oecd.org/tax/part-1-of-report-to-g20-dwg-on-the-impact-of-beps-in-low-income-countries.pdf

OECD. 2016a "Multilateral convention to implement tax treaty related measures to prevent [base erosion and profit shifting] BEPS." OECD, Paris. Accessed 25 July 2019. www.oecd.org/tax/treaties/multilateral-convention-to-implement-tax-treaty-related-measures-to-prevent-beps.htm

OECD. 2016b. *Revenue statistics in Africa.* Paris: OECD. https://doi.org/10.1787/2617653x

Olson M. 1963. *The economics of the wartime shortage: A history of British food supplies in the Napoleonic war and in world wars I and II.* Durham: Duke University Press.

Omotola J. and Sailu H. 2009. "Foreign aid, debt relief and Africa's development: Problems and prospects." *South African Journal of International Affairs* 16(1): 87-102.

Ormrod W. M., Bonney M. and Bonney R. (Eds.) 1999. *Crises, revolutions and self-sustained growth: Essays in European fiscal history, 1130-1830.* Stamford: Shaun Tyas. https://books.google.co.ke/books?id=xCaaAAAAIAAJ

Owino J. 2019, Jul 8. "Africa free trade zone to be operational July 2020." Capital Business. Accessed 8 October 2019. www.capitalfm.co.ke/business/2019/07/africa-free-trade-zone-to-be-operational-july-2020

Partlow J. 2013. "The necessity of complexity in the tax system." *Wyoming Law Review* 13(1): 303-334. https://repository.uwyo.edu/cgi/viewcontent.cgi?referer=https://www.google.com/&httpsredir=1&article=1048&context=wlr

Pfister M. 2009. *Taxation for investment and development: An overview of policy challenges in Africa.* For the ministerial meeting and expert roundtable of the NEPAD-OECD Africa Investment Initiative. Paris: OECD. www.oecd.org/investment/investmentfordevelopment/43966821.pdf

Picciotto S. 2019. "The interactions of national and international tax law and the Kenya-Mauritius tax treaty." *Journal on Financing for Development* 1(1): 1-32. http://uonjournals.uonbi.ac.ke/ojs/index.php/ffd/issue/view/54

Prebble J. 1998. "Should tax legislation be written from a principles and purpose point of view or a precise and detailed point of view?" *British Tax Review* (2): 112-123.

Prest A. R. 1979. "The structure and reform of direct taxation." *The Economic Journal* vol 89 (June), no 354: 243-260.

PricewaterhouseCoopers. 2018. "Namibia tax reference and rate card 2019." Accessed 7 September 2019. www.pwc.com/na/en/assets/pdf/namibia-tax-reference-and-rate-card-2019.pdf

Puntland Development Research Center. 2004. "Report on socioeconomic assessment of Puntland.": Puntland Development Research Center, Garowe, Somalia. Accessed 20

August 2019. www.jccp.gr.jp/ src/sc2334/2 PDRC-Socio economic report.pdf

Republic of France. 1789. Declaration of the rights of man and of the citizen.

Republic of France. 1793. Constitution.

Republic of Guinea. 1990. Code général des impôts.

Republic of Guinea. 2006. Local government code.

Republic of Guinea. 2010. Constitution. Accessed 25 May 2018. www.gouvernement.gov.gn/images/constitution-guineenne-de-2010.pdf

Republic of Guinea. 2017. "Guide du citoyen : loi de finances 2017." Accessed 27 August 2019. www.mbudget.gov.gn/index.php/guide-du-citoyen-lf2017

Republic of Guinea. 2018. Institut national de la statistique. Accessed 25 May 2018. www.stat-guinee.org

Republic of Guinea. 2019. "Guide du citoyen : loi de finances 2019." Accessed 7 October 2019. www.mbudget.gov.gn/index.php/guide-du-citoyen-lf2019

Republic of Kenya. 1988. Income tax act (Cap 470).

Republic of Kenya. 1995. Kenya revenue authority act.

Republic of Kenya. 2010. Constitution.

Republic of Kenya. 2012. Income tax act (Cap 470). kenyalaw.org:8181/exist/kenyalex/actview.xql?actid=CAP.%20470

Republic of Kenya. 2013. Value added tax act (no. 35). www.kra.go.ke and http://cn.investmentkenya.com/wp-content/uploads/2018/10/ValueAddedTax ActNo35of2013.pdf

Republic of Kenya. 2015. Tax procedures act (no 29). www.kra.go.ke

Republic of Kenya. 2017, Jul 21. "Community of Kenyans of Asian heritage recognised as Kenya's 44th tribe." In a special issue of *The Kenya Gazette*, Vol. CXIX-No.102.

Republic of Kenya. 2018. Income tax bill.

Republic of Mauritius. 2002. Environment protection act.

Republic of Mauritius. 2007. *Mauritius Revenue Authority annual report.*

Republic of Namibia. 2016. Ministry of Finance. www.mof.gov.na

Republic of Namibia. 2017. "Revenue expenditure and budget balancing." Accessed 25 May 2018. www.mof.gov.na

Republic of Rwanda. 2003 (revised 2015). Constitution. Accessed 27 August 2019.
www.constituteproject.org/constitution/Rwanda_2015?lang=en

Republic of Rwanda. 2005. Income tax act (law no. 16/2005 of 18/08/2005).
http://admin.theiguides.org/Media/Documents/DirectTaxesLaw2005.pdf

Republic of Senegal. 2001. Constitution de la République du Sénégal.

Republic of Senegal. 2010. "Plan Sénégal émergent, résumé." Accessed 20 July 2016
www.sec.gouv.sn/sites/default/files/Resume%20Plan%20Senegal%20Emergent.pdf

Republic of Tanzania. 2013. Constitution. In Swahili: www.asclibrary.nl/docs/332790886-001.pdf

Republic of Tanzania. 2016a, Jan. "Budget execution report for the first half of the fiscal year 2016/17." Ministry of Finance and Planning. Accessed 15 May 2017.
www.mof.go.tz/mofdocs/budget/Budget%20Execution%20Report/Budget%20Execution%20Report%20(Mid%20Year)%20July-%20December%202016%20Final.pdf

Republic of Tanzania. 2016b, Jun. "Speech by the minister for finance and planning, Hon. Dr. Philip I. Mpango (MP), introducing to the national assembly, the estimates of government revenue and expenditure for fiscal year 2016/17." Accessed 15 May 2017.
www.tra.go.tz/images/uploads/Laws/BUDGETSPEECHFINAL.2016.pdf

Republic of Tanzania. 2017a. Income tax act (Cap 332). See tax acts here: www.tra.go.tz/index.php/laws

Republic of Tanzania. 2017b. "National five year development plan 2016/17 - 2020/21: Nurturing industrialization for economic transformation and human development." Ministry of Finance and Planning. Accessed 24 August 2019.
www.mof.go.tz/mofdocs/msemaji/Five%202016_17_2020_21.pdf

Republic of Tanzania. 2017c. "SEZ/EPZ program." Accessed 15 May 2017. www.epza.go.tz/invest.php?p=232

Republic of Uganda. 2014. Tax procedures code act. Accessed 4 September 2019.
https://ugandalaws.com/Pdf/Act%2014%20of%202014.pdf

Ricardo D. and Sraffa P. 1962. *The works and correspondence of David Ricardo*. Cambridge: Cambridge University Press. From 2004, see Indianapolis: Liberty Fund document at
http://ricardo.ecn.wfu.edu/~cottrell/ecn265/Principles.pdf

Roberts J. 2003. "Poverty reduction outcomes in education and health: Public expenditure and aid." Working paper 210. Overseas Development Institute, London.
www.odi.org/sites/odi.org.uk/files/odi-assets/publications-opinion-files/2450.pdf

Rotuk R. 2016, Jun 7. "Government should be clear on law to allow or disallow tax avoidance." *The East African*.

Sabine B. E. V. 1991. *A short history of taxation*. London: Butterworths.

Schauer F. 1991. *Playing by the rules: A philosophical examination of rule-based decision-making in law and in life*. Oxford: Clarendon.

Schumpeter J. A. 1942. *Capitalism, socialism and democracy*. New York: Harper.

Schuyler M. 2014. "The impact of Piketty's wealth tax on the poor, the rich, and the middle class." Accessed 23 May 2016.
https://taxfoundation.org/impact-piketty-s-wealth-tax-poor-rich-and-middle-class

Seabrooke L. and Wigan D. 2017. "The governance of global wealth chains." *Review of International Political Economy* 24(1): 1-29.
https://doi.org/10.1080/09692290.2016.1268189

Seligman E. R. A. 1908. "Progressive taxation in theory and practice (2nd ed.)." *American Economic Association Quarterly*, 3rd series, 9(4): 1-334.
https://archive.org/details/progressivetaxat00seliuoft/page/n3

Shapiro S. J. 2007. "The Hart-Dworkin debate: A short guide for the perplexed." Yale University Law School.
https://dx.doi.org/10.2139/ssrn.968657

Shere L. 1948. "Taxation and inflation control." *American Economic Review* 38(5): 843-856. www.jstor.org/stable/1811695

Simon K. W. 1987. "Tax simplification and justice." 36 *Tax Notes* 93: 99-100.

Smith A. 1977. *An inquiry into the nature and causes of the wealth of nations.* London: Dutton. First published 1776. See: http://files.libertyfund.org/files/220/0141-02_Bk.pdf and www.ibiblio.org/ml/libri/s/SmithA_WealthNations_s.pdf

Solether B. and Coleman S. 1989. "Flowcharts for section 469." 44 *Tax Notes* 1254.

Sornarajah M. 2010. *The international law on foreign investment* (3rd ed.). New York: Cambridge University Press. www.worldcat.org/title/international-law-on-foreign-investment/oclc/1040292344/viewport

The Star. 2018, May 9. "NYS hit by fresh Sh10 billion scandal." Accessed 2 November 2018. www.the-star.co.ke/news/2018/05/12/nys-hit-by-fresh-sh10-billion-scandal_c1757639

Steele D. 1975. "The theory of the dual economy and African entrepreneurship in Kenya." *Journal of Development Studies* 12(1): 18-38. https://doi.org/10.1080/00220387508421558

Stiglitz J. E. 2014. "Reforming taxation to promote growth and equity." Roosevelt Institute white paper. Accessed 29 September 2019. https://rooseveltinstitute.org/reforming-taxation-promote-growth-and-equity

Taussig F. W. 1911. *Principles of economics.* New York: Macmillan.

Tax Justice Network. 2018. Financial secrecy index. Tax Justice Network, Chesham, United Kingdom. Accessed 7 October 2019. https://financialsecrecyindex.com/en/introduction/fsi-2018-results

Thiankolu M. K. 2019. "Using public procurement as a tool of economic and social development policy in Kenya: Lessons from the United States and South Africa." *Journal on Financing for Development* 1(1): 97-129. http://uonjournals.uonbi.ac.ke/ojs/index.php/ffd/issue/view/54

Thornhill J. 2018. "Data as a commodity." In *What to tax: Perspectives on tax are changing; tax is changing perspectives* (pp. 18-19). KMPG International. Accessed 1 September 2019. https://assets.kpmg/content/dam/kpmg/xx/pdf/2018/10/what-to-tax-web.pdf

Tickle D. 2018. "Can tax law really be made simpler?" *GAA Accounting*, journal of the Global Accounting Alliance. www.gaaaccounting.com/can-tax-law-really-be-made-simpler

Tiffen M., Mortimore M. and Gichuki F. 1994. *More people, less erosion: Environmental recovery in Kenya.* Chichester: Wiley. https://books.google.com/books?isbn=9780471941439

Transparency International. 2017. Corruption perceptions index. Accessed 27 August 2017. www.transparency.org/news/feature/corruption_perceptions_i ndex_2017

Tutt N. 1985. *The history of tax avoidance: An update of the 1980s classic The tax raiders.* London: Wisedene.

UNCTAD. 2012. *Report on the implementation of the investment policy review of Rwanda.* Geneva: UNCTAD. https://investmentpolicy.unctad.org/publications/107/report-on-the-implementation-of-the-investment-policy-review-of-rwanda

UNCTAD. 2018. *Achieving the sustainable development goals in the least developed countries: A compendium of policy options.* Geneva: UNCTAD. unctad.org/en/pages/PublicationWebflyer.aspx?publicationid=2131

UNCTAD. 2019. *Economic development in Africa report 2019: Made in Africa rules of origin for enhanced intra-African trade.* Geneva: UNCTAD. Accessed 27 August 2019. https://unctad.org/en/pages/PublicationWebflyer.aspx?public ationid=2463

UNDESA. 2015. "Financing sustainable development and developing sustainable finance: A DESA briefing note on the Addis Ababa action agenda." UNDESA, New York. Accessed 7 October 2019. www.un.org/esa/ffd/ffd3/wp-content/uploads/sites/2/2015/07/DESA-Briefing-Note-Addis-Action-Agenda.pdf

UNECA. 1990. African charter for popular participation in development and transformation. International conference in Arusha, Tanzania on popular participation in the recovery and development process in Africa. https://repository.uneca.org/handle/10855/5673

UNECA. 2018. *Africa sustainable development report: Towards a transformed and resilient continent.* Addis Ababa: UNECA. Accessed 29 August 2019. www.uneca.org/publications/2018-africa-sustainable-development-report

UNESCO. 2018. "R&D data release." http://uis.unesco.org/en/news/rd-data-release

United Nations. 1945. Statute of the international court of justice. http://legal.un.org/avl/pdf/ha/sicj/icj_statute_e.pdf and https://treaties.un.org/Pages/ViewDetails.aspx?src=TREATY &mtdsg_no=I-3&chapter=1&clang=_en

United Nations. 2000a. Millennium development goals. www.undp.org/content/undp/en/home/sdgoverview/mdg_goals.html and www.who.int/topics/millennium_development_goals/about/en

United Nations. 2015a. *2030 agenda for sustainable development.* New York: United Nations. Accessed 25 August 2019. https://sustainabledevelopment.un.org/post2015/transforming ourworld

United Nations. 2015b. "Financing for development." Accessed 29 July 2019. www.un.org/sustainabledevelopment/financing-for-development

United Nations. 2019. Africa SDG index and dashboards. Accessed 30 July 2019. See https://africasdgindex.org

United States Embassy in Nigeria. 2012. "Nigeria fact sheet." Accessed 25 June 2019. https://photos.state.gov/libraries/nigeria/487468/pdfs/Nigeri a%20overview%20Fact%20Sheet.pdf

Von Kommer V. and Waris A. 2013. "Key building blocks for effective tax systems in developing countries utilizing the theory of the development of the fiscal state." *Bulletin for International Taxation* 65(11): 620-636.

Wagana D. M., Iravo M. A., Nzulwa J. D. and Kihoro J. M. 2016. "Effect of financial and political decentralization on service delivery in county governments in Kenya." *International Journal of Academic Research in Business and Social Sciences* 6(6): 304-320. http://ir.jkuat.ac.ke/handle/123456789/3300

Wagner A. 1880. *Finanzwissenschaft.*[385] Leipzig: C. F. Winter. E-book of 1890 (2nd ed.) is free: https://books.google.co.ke/books?id=vW83AQAAIAAJ&pg=PR3&redir_esc=y#v=onepage&q&f=false

Waris A. 2007. "Taxation without principles: A historical analysis of the Kenyan taxation system." *Kenya Law Review* 1: 272-304. http://erepository.uonbi.ac.ke/handle/11295/38764

Waris A., Kohonen M., Ranguma J. and Mosioma A. 2009.*Taxation and state building in Kenya: Enhancing revenue capacity to advance human welfare.* Nairobi: Tax Justice Network Africa. www.academia.edu/1088013/Taxation_and_State_Building_in_Kenya_Enhancing_Revenue_Capacity_to_Advance_Human_W elfare

Waris A. and Kohonen M. 2011. "Linking taxation to the realisation of the millennium development goals in Africa." Paper presented at the Development Studies Association conference on rethinking development in an age of scarcity and uncertainty, University of York, York, UK, 19-22 September. Program accessed 7 September 2019: www.devstud.org.uk/conferences/2011

Waris A. and Murangwa H. 2012. "Utilising tax literacy and societal confidence in a state: The Rwandan model." www.academia.edu/2419611/Utilising_Tax_Literacy_and_Soci etal_Confidence_in_a_State_The_Rwandan_Model

Waris A. 2013a. *Tax and development: Solving Kenya's fiscal crisis through human rights – a case study of Kenya's constituency development fund.* Nairobi: LawAfrica.

Waris A. 2013b. "Taxation and state legitimacy in Kenya." In J Leaman and A Waris (Eds.), *Tax justice and the political economy of global capitalism, 1945 to the present* (chapter 7, pp. 151-180). Oxford: Berghahn. https://books.google.com/books?isbn=9780857458827

Waris A. 2013c. "Taxing intra-company transfers: The law and its application in Rwanda" *Bulletin for International Taxation* 67(12).

---

[385] a "majestic study of the theory of public finance" according to www.hetwebsite.net/het/profiles/wagner.htm

www.academia.edu/7077908/Taxing_Intra-
Company_Transfers_The_Law_and_Its_Application_in_Rwanda

Waris A. 2014a. "Rwanda: Understanding transfer pricing." *International Transfer Pricing Journal* 21(1): 80-82.

Waris A. 2014b. "Tax haven or international financial centre? The case of Kenya." U4 anti-corruption resource centre brief, Chr. Michelsen Institute, Bergen, Norway. www.cmi.no/publications/5242-tax-haven-or-international-financial-centre

Waris A. 2014c. "Tax literacy in developing countries: A Rwandan case study." PowerPoint presentation for OECD session on Measuring progress: Special focus on tax morale and taxpayer education. www.oecd.org/ctp/49836943.pdf

Waris A. 2015. "Delineating a rights-based fiscal social contract using African fiscal constitutions." *East African Law Journal* 68-98. See www.academia.edu/21766421/Delineating_a_Rights-based_Fiscal_Social_Contract_Using_African_Fiscal_Constitutions

Waris A. and Latif L. A. 2015. "Towards establishing fiscal legitimacy through settled fiscal principles in global health financing." *Health Care Analysis* 23(4): 376-390. https://doi.org/10.1007/s10728-015-0305-z

Waris A. 2017a. "How Kenya has implemented and adjusted to the changes in international transfer pricing regulations: 1920-2016." Working paper 69. International Centre for Tax and Development, Brighton, UK. www.ictd.ac/publication/how-kenya-has-implemented-and-adjusted-to-the-changes-in-international-transfer-pricing-regulations-1920-2016

Waris A. 2017b. "Legitimising the tax collection through participatory budgeting." *East African Law Journal* 59-71.

Waris A. 2017c "Measures undertaken by African countries to counter illicit financial flows: Unpacking the African Report of the high-level panel on illicit financial flows." In J. Owens, R. C. D. Franzsen, R. McDonell and J. Amos (Eds.), *Inter-agency cooperation and good tax governance in Africa* (pp. 15-42). Pretoria: Pretoria University Law Press. www.pulp.up.ac.za/legal-compilations/inter-agency-cooperation-and-good-tax-governance-in-africa

Waris A. 2018a. "Developing fiscal legitimacy by building state-societal trust in African countries." *Journal of Tax Administration* 4(2): 103-118. http://jota.website/index.php/JoTA/article/view/199

Waris A. 2018b. "Tax compliance-eine: das befolgen steuerlicher vorschriften, eine afrikanische perspektive." *Amosinternational* 12(4): 34-38. www.amosinternational.de/magazine/issue-2018-4

Waris A. 2019. "Towards an African and Kenyan philosophy of fiscal legitimacy." *Journal on Financing for Development* 1(1): 33-46. http://uonjournals.uonbi.ac.ke/ojs/index.php/ffd/issue/view/54

Waris, A. and Magara W. 2019. African revenue and expenditure map. Accessed 30 September 2019. https://cfs.uonbi.ac.ke/revenue_expenditure.html

Waris A., Maina M. and Magara W. 2019. Dataset on extractives and their tax rates. www.uonbi.ac.ke

Waris A., Muendo E. and Magara W. 2019. Budgets dataset. www.uonbi.ac.ke

Waris A., Waridah M. and Magara W. 2019. Debt, aid and state-owned enterprises dataset. www.uonbi.ac.ke

WikiLeaks. 2015. The WikiLeaks files. Accessed 30 July 2019. See https://wikileaks.org/What-is-WikiLeaks.html

Wolfers L. 2018. "Indirect taxes on the digital economy: What to tax?" In *What to tax: Perspectives on tax are changing; tax is changing perspectives* (pp. 64-69). KMPG International. Accessed 1 September 2019. https://assets.kpmg/content/dam/kpmg/xx/pdf/2018/10/what-to-tax-web.pdf

World Bank. 2012, Nov 9. "Tax modernisation project: Implementation completion and results (ICR) review by Independent Evaluation Group (IEG)." World Bank, Washington, DC. Accessed 4 September 2019. http://projects.worldbank.org/P100314/tax-modernization-project?lang=en

World Bank. 2017a. "Rwanda economic update." World Bank, Washington, DC.

World Bank. 2017b. "Where we work - Tanzania." Accessed 15 May 2017. www.worldbank.org/en/country/tanzania/overview

World Bank. 2017c. "Data - Tanzania - Poverty headcount ratio at $1.90 a day (2011 PPP) (% of population)." Accessed 15 May 2017.
http://data.worldbank.org/indicator/SI.POV.DDAY?locations=TZ

World Bank. 2018. *Doing business: Reforming to create jobs* (15ᵗʰ ed.). *Comparing business regulation for domestic firms in 190 economies.* Washington, DC: World Bank. www.doingbusiness.org/content/dam/doingBusiness/media/Annual-Reports/English/DB2018-Full-Report.pdf

Zubeldia G. E. 2017. "Introducing VAT in the Gulf states: Development affects not only domestic supplies of goods and services but also purchases made from unestablished suppliers." Accessed 29 July 2019. https://taxexecutive.org/introducing-vat-in-the-gulf-states

* not cited directly

Court cases

Commissioner of Income Tax v Westmont Power (K) Ltd [2006] eKLR http://kenyalaw.org/caselaw/cases/view/14749

Commissioners of Inland Revenue v Scottish Central Electric Power Company [1931] 15 Tax Cases 761

Commissioner of Inland Revenue (CIR) v Simpson [1949] (4) SA 678 (A)

Inland Revenue Commissioners v Duke of Westminster [1936] AC 1; 19 Tax Cases 490

Karen and Langata Residents Association v The City Council of Nairobi and Another [1999] eKLR

Keroche Industries Limited v Kenya Revenue Authority & 5 Others [2007] eKLR

Khambaita v Commissioner of Income Tax [1954] 21 East African Court of Appeal (EACA) 16

Mangin v Inland Revenue Commissioner [1971] AC 739 (PC)

Matthews v Chicory Board [1938] 60 Common Law Reports (CLR) 263

Pepper (Inspector of Taxes) v Hart [1992] UKHL and AC 593 and STC 898

Republic v Commissioner of Domestic Taxes (Large Taxpayers Office) Ex parte Barclays Bank of Kenya Limited [2015] eKLR

Republic v Kenya Revenue Authority Exparte Bata Shoe Company (Kenya) Limited [2014] eKLR www.kenyalaw.org/caselaw/cases/view/95119

Savage v CIR [1951] 18 SATC 1

Silver Chain Limited v Commissioner Income Tax & 3 others [2016] eKLR

Singh v Commissioner for the South African Revenue Service [2003 Mar 31] Supreme Court of Appeal of South Africa ZASCA www.saflii.org/za/cases/ZASCA/2003/31.html

Unilever Kenya Limited v The Commissioner General, Kenya Revenue Authority [2005] eKLR

Williamson v Commissioner of Income Tax [1955] 22 EACA 227

W. T. Ramsay Limited v Inland Revenue Commissioner [1981 Mar 12] HL

Appendices

Appendix A: Screen capture from the African revenue and expenditure map dataset housed at University of Nairobi

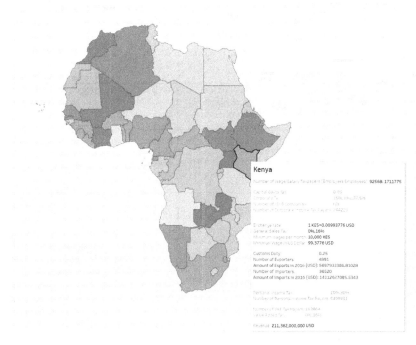

Source: Waris and Magara (2019)[386]

---

[386] When referencing the entire compiled data, cite as Waris and Magara (2019), however, when referring to the individual components of data, the references are as follows: African Union Department of Economic Affairs, Waris and Magara (2019) for the trade dataset; ATAF, Waris and Magara (2019) for the taxpayer dataset; Waris, Waridah and Magara (2019) for the debt, aid and state-owned enterprises dataset.

Appendix B: Adapted Ormrod and Bonney model of developmental stages of the fiscal state

Indicator	Tribute State characteristics	Domain State characteristics	Tax State characteristics	Fiscal State characteristics
Financial theory	Beginning of a general theory	Relatively undeveloped theory	Mercantilism and 'cameralist'	Highly developed theories
Form of government	'Predatory' peripatetic rulers (dynastic) or tribes	Personal, few limits in decision making	Highly developed institutions and legal procedures	Precise credit and tax legislation and 'fiscal constitution'
Central administration	Kinsmen, marital allies and clients of the ruler	Small staff in more primitive forms	Well staffed; specialised departments with defined authority	Sophisticated organisation of departments; planning; administration
Local administration	High levels of local autonomy but with the sanction of royal intervention and/or punishment		Regularly controlled by central government	Highly developed control by the centre
Officeholders	Royal kinsmen and families of rank, sometimes Church officials		Professionally trained personnel	
			Many of these may still be holders of venal offices	Appointments more or less on merit and presumed competence
State responsibilities			Active influence on and regulation of all aspects of life	
Maintenance of law and order				Process of regulation may include elements of social engineering
Method of financing	Mix of payments in money and in kind		Mainly monetization	High levels of monetization
Public finance	Plunder and extortion; surplus produced by those colonized	Surplus produced by domain or other regalian rights; exploitation	Increasing importance of taxation	Precise planning of taxation with reference to the economy and public opinion
Defence	Not heavily related to scale of military effort			
	Reliance on booty and conquests to meet expenditure		Increasing size of armies, technological developments, and simultaneous military and naval armament	

Indicator	Tribute State characteristics	Domain State characteristics	Tax State characteristics	Fiscal State characteristics
		In more advanced systems, scaling down of household costs and all military costs (except for emergencies) in relation to predicted income	Escalating military costs which spiral out of control in periods of sustained warfare; costs of debt servicing acute in periods of wartime; other costs may be curtailed	Leads to the development of 'fiscal-military' states, some of which gain superpower status; 'modern' sophisticated states may incur considerable levels of expenditure on health, social security and other 'welfare' costs for the population
Revenues	Taxes an infrequent aid, limited to specific purposes; exactions and extortions play an important role; systematic debasement of the coinage in wartime		Regular direct and indirect taxes, no longer limited to specific purposes; exactions and extortion play little or no role; debasement of the coinage, even in wartime, becomes unusual; attempts to unify the tax structure, avoiding regressive taxes and relating the burden of taxation much more closely to the sources of wealth	Direct and indirect taxes of a highly sophisticated kind, with income taxes, property taxes and other duties levied with a view to maximizing fiscal efficiency and assisting economic development; unified tax structure with greater emphasis on 'progression'; levels of economic growth and inflation play an increasing part in taxpayers' expectations
		'Renewal' of coinage in peacetime		
Credit structure	Some short-term loans, but lack of a settled structure for public credit; weak private finance corporations	Short-term bridging loans against interest in kind or mortgaging of domain land; some reliance on external, urban credit markets	Sophisticated credit structures, with variable but often low rates of interest	
Role in economy	Circulation of accumulated precious metals and foodstuffs	Independent, active and profitable producer	Taxation as means of participation in profits made by subjects	

Indicator	Tribute State characteristics	Domain State characteristics	Tax State characteristics	Fiscal State characteristics
Economic policy	Colonization and slavery may assume importance; securing of food supply fundamental to the system	Market intervention to keep prices down; securing of food supply fundamental to the system	Market supervision; subsidies for potentially profitable enterprises in trade and industry; 'mercantilist' intervention in trading policies between states; acquisition of overseas empires for trade and raw materials	At times of internal crisis in wartime, highly interventionist role in the economy; in peacetime, more laissez-faire approach to trade and industry, although regulation remains the norm; crucial role in influencing interest rates and the money supply; possible manipulation of inflation in the interests of government borrowing; collapse of control and 'hyperinflation' in other states
Public enterprises	None except perhaps the army itself	Agricultural and mining enterprises in conjunction with domain	Monopolies with guaranteed supply and fixed prices; supervision of grain supply and other commodities during shortage; royal or state sponsored, trading companies	Growth of the state sector as the state assumes greater responsibilities; rise in costs of certain parts of the state sector (e.g. health and social security) help ensure self-sustained growth in the size of the state sector
Political participation	Restricted to a small number of families	Little and infrequent activity of the estates of the realm	Initially on the increase; authorization and administration of taxes; later limited or removed by 'absolute' rulers	Highly variable, tendency towards participation because of the reliance on and sophistication of credit structures
Social consequences	Negligible; stabilization of	Compulsion to increase productivity		

Indicator	Tribute State characteristics	Domain State characteristics	Tax State characteristics	Fiscal State characteristics
	agricultural economy except in wartime; exemptions and concessions for privileged groups	Social disciplining; redistribution of purchasing power		Exemptions and concessions for privileged groups largely removed in the interests of fiscal efficiency, unless groups benefit from special tax or social security advantages; relatively small tax changes can assume electoral significance in democracies
Statistics	Rare; surveys only to assist estimation of output except in more advanced systems; difficulty in establishing any sort of balance sheet in less advanced systems	Frequent productivity surveys; tax registers of houses, landowners, tradespeople and artisans; sophisticated accounting		Statistical sophistication; tendency towards frequent production of and reliance on statistics; monthly figures and decennial census of population
Causes of instability / precipitants of change in the system	Civil war, foreign invasion, collapse of control over outlying regions – all potentially leading to the overthrow of the state, and with it, the prevailing fiscal system	Active military conflict with larger armies in an era of technological change and increasing military costs might overwhelm all but the most sophisticated domain states; the absence of reliable loan and tax income becomes crucial in a long conflict	High debt servicing costs or debt-revenue ratios leading to quasi-bankruptcy; inability to renege on public debt owing to its contractual nature; political impasse between the crown and powerful sectional groups over the nature of a revised 'fiscal constitution'; potential overthrow of the state	Ideologically inspired attempts to 'roll back' the state have yet to prove successful in the long term; inherent tendency of health and social security payments to rise with increased life expectancy; technological costs of warfare prohibitive for sustained conflict other than with nuclear or biological weapons
Human rights and social welfare	Limited to security rights	Broader rights like fair trial begin to emerge	Civil and political or	Full access of all rights

Indicator	Tribute State characteristics	Domain State characteristics	Tax State characteristics	Fiscal State characteristics
			economic and social accessed	
Fiscal literacy	Little or no literacy or financial literacy	Increased literacy but little financial literacy	Increased financial literacy	Full and complete financial literacy
Tax administration	Non-existent	Limited and oppressive	Growing but oppressive	Well organized and not oppressive

Source: Adapted from Ormrod, Bonney and Bonney (1999)

Appendix C: Publicly available data on state-owned enterprises, as of December 2018

	Country	Government business	Shares held
1.	Algeria	Air Algérie SpA	100%
		Sonatrach	100%
		Radio Algeria	100%
		Somatel-Liebherr	51%
2.	Angola	TAAG Angola Airlines	100%
		Sonangol	100%
		Catoca Diamond Mine	32.8%
3.	Benin	Banque internationale du Bénin (BIBE)	8.2%
4.	Botswana	Air Botswana	100%
		Bank of Botswana	100%
5.	Burkina Faso	Air Burkina	5%
6.	Burundi	Air Burundi	100%
		Burundi National Radio and Television	100%
7.	Cameroon	Camair-Co	100%
8.	Cape Verde	TACV Cabo Verde Airlines	100%
		Bank of Cape Verde	100%
9.	Central African Republic	Commercial Bank Centrafrique	100%
10.	Chad	Tchadia Airlines	51%
11.	Comoros	Central Bank of Comoros	100%
12.	Congo, Brazza	National Oil Company	100%
13.	Cote d'Ivoire	Air Côte d'Ivoire	58%
14.	Democratic Republic of Congo	Ge Camines	100%
15.	Djibouti	Doraleh Container Terminal	100%
16.	Egypt	Egypt Air	100%
		Sono Cairo	100%
17.	Equatorial Guinea	GEPetrol	20%
18.	Eritrea	Central Bank of Eritrea	100%
19.	Ethiopia	Ethiopian Airlines	100%
		Ethiopia Telecom	100%
20.	Gabon	Société nationale pétrolière gabonaise	100%
21.	Gambia	Gambia Civil Aviation Authority	100%
22.	Ghana	Volta River Authority	100%
23.	Guinea	Compagnie des bauxites de Guinée[387]	49%

---

[387] https://fr.wikipedia.org/wiki/Listes_d%27entreprises_de_la_Guinée

24.	Guinea Bissau	Electricidade e Aguas da Guine-Bissau (EAGB)	100%
25.	Kenya	Kenya Airways	29.8%
		Kenya Broadcasting Corporation	100%
26.	Lesotho	Central Bank of Lesotho	100%
27.	Liberia	Central Bank of Liberia	100%
		Liberia Telecommunications Authority	100%
28.	Libya	Libyan Airways	100%
		Libyan Jamahiriya Broadcasting Corporation	100%
29.	Madagascar	Air Madagascar	89.56%
30.	Malawi	Malawian Airlines	51%
31.	Mali	Office de Radiodiffusion-Télévision du Mali (ORTM)	100%
32.	Mauritania	National Bank of Mauritania	50%
33.	Mauritius	Air Mauritius	100%
34.	Morocco	Royal Air Maroc	53.94%
35.	Mozambique	LAM-Linhas Aeres de Mozambique	100%
36.	Namibia	Air Namibia	100%
37.	Niger	Société des mines de l'air (SOMAIR)	36.6%
38.	Nigeria	Garden City Radio 89.9	100%
39.	Rwanda	Rwanda Air	99%
40.	Senegal	Société nationale d'électricité du Sénégal (Senelec)	100%
41.	Seychelles	Seychelles Petroleum Company Ltd (SEYPEC)	100%
42.	Sierra Leone	Sierra Leone Commercial Bank	100%
43.	Somalia	Somalia Petroleum Corporation	100%
44.	South Africa	South African Airways	100%
		South African Express	100%
		ESKOM	100%
		Transnet	100%
45.	South Sudan	Eden Commercial Bank	100%
46.	Sudan	Sudan Airways	51%
47.	Swaziland	Sovereign Wealth Fund (SWF), Tibiyo Taka Ngwane	100%
48.	Tanzania	Air Tanzania	100%
49.	Togo	La Poste du Togo	100%
50.	Tunisia	Tunisair	74%
51.	Uganda	Uganda Development Bank Ltd	100%
52.	Zambia	Zambia Daily Mail	100%

53.	Zimbabwe	Air Zimbabwe	100%
		Agricultural Bank of Zimbabwe	100%
		TelOne Zimbabwe	100%

Source: Waris and Waridah[388]

---

[388] This table is a compilation by Waris, A. and Waridah, M. (2019) of "Publicly available data on state-owned enterprises." Sources: Africa-EU Renewable Energy Cooperation Programme (RECP) (2018); African Airline Association (2018); Bank of Botswana (2018); BBC News (2019); Business Advantage PNG (2019); Central Bank of Lesotho (2019); Central Bank of Liberia (2019); Centre for aviation (2019); Corporate Finance Institute (2018); Department of Public Enterprises - South Africa (2019); Discogs regarding Sono Cairo (2019); *Entreprise nationale des matériels de travaux publics* (2018); Europa Publications, Africa South of the Sahara (2004); Export Governance of Congo (2019); Export.gov - Swaziland (2019); Garden city 89.9FM (2019); Gurtong Trust (2019); ITU Telecom World (2018); Japan Times (2018); Journal of Commerce (2019); KBC News - Kenya's National Broadcasting Corporation (2019); La poste (2019); Macauhub (2018); Malawi tourism (2019); Mining Africa (2019); Mining Technology (2018); Nations encyclopedia (2019); NewsAfrica Guinee (2019); Pindula regarding TelOne (2019); Press reference (2018); Psychology Press (2003); Reuters (2018); Revolvy (2019); Seychelles Petroleum Company Limited (SEYPEC, 2018); Sonatrach (2018); State Enterprises Commission - Ghana (2019); Uganda Development Bank Limited (2019); U. S. Department of State (2018); West African Bankers' Association (2018); World Investment News (2019); and Zambian Watchdog (2018).

Appendix D: Publicly available data on aid to African countries, as of July 2019

	Country	Aid amount	Funding source	Year
1.	Algeria	€9 million	EU humanitarian	2018
		$10 million	USAID	2017
2.	Angola	$76 million	USAID	2017
3.	Benin	$419 million	USAID	2017
4.	Botswana	$41 million	USAID	2017
5.	Burkina Faso	€16.1 million	EU humanitarian	2018
		$82 million	USAID	2017
6.	Burundi	€13 million	EU humanitarian	2018
		$68 million	USAID	2017
7.	Cameroon	€19.4 million	EU humanitarian	2018
		$121 million	USAID	2017
8.	Cape Verde	$962,000	USAID	2017
9.	Central African Republic	€26.5 million	EU humanitarian	2018
		$118 million	USAID	2017
10.	Chad	€54.7 million	EU humanitarian	2018
		$116 million	USAID	2017
11.	Comoros	$1.2 million	USAID	2017
12.	Congo, Brazza	$36 million	USAID	2017
13.	Cote d'Ivoire	$164 million	USAID	2017
14.	Democratic Republic of Congo	€77 million	EU humanitarian	2018
		$494 million	USAID	2017
15.	Djibouti	$31 million	USAID	2017
16.	Egypt	$1.3 billion	US foreign aid	2016
		$1.5 billion	USAID	2017
17.	Equatorial Guinea	$76,000	USAID	2017
18.	Eritrea	$130,000	USAID	2017
19.	Ethiopia	€63 million	EU humanitarian	2018
		$967million	US foreign aid	2016
		$1.1 billion	USAID	2017
20.	Gabon	$2.1 million	USAID	2017
21.	Gambia	$19 million	USAID	2017
22.	Ghana	$184 million	USAID	2017
23.	Guinea	$65 million	USAID	2017
24.	Guinea Bissau	$1.7 million	USAID	2017
25.	Kenya	€11.5 million	EU humanitarian	2018
		$894 million	US foreign aid	2016
		1.1 billion	USAID	2017
26.	Lesotho	$52 million	USAID	2017
27.	Liberia	$212 million	USAID	2017
28.	Libya	$79 million	USAID	2017
29.	Madagascar	$91 million	USAID	2016
30.	Malawi	$304 million	USAID	2017

	Country	Aid amount	Funding source	Year
31.	Mali	€35.35 million	EU humanitarian	2018
		$230 million	USAID	2017
32.	Mauritania	€16.4 million	EU humanitarian	2018
		$17 million	USAID	2017
33.	Mauritius	$450,000	USAID	2017
34.	Morocco	$490 million	USAID	2017
35.	Mozambique	$580 million	USAID	2017
36.	Namibia	$54 million	USAID	2017
37.	Niger	€32.4million	EU humanitarian	2018
		$173 million	USAID	2017
38.	Nigeria	€48.3 million	EU humanitarian	2018
		$852million	USAID	2017
39.	Rwanda	$170 million	USAID	2017
40.	Senegal	€1 million	EU humanitarian	2018
		$197 million	USAID	2017
41.	Seychelles	$1.3 million	USAID	2017
42.	Sierra Leone	$62 million	USAID	2017
43.	Somalia	€89 million	EU humanitarian	2018
		$584 million	USAID	2017
44.	South Africa	$511 million	USAID	2017
45.	South Sudan	€45 million	EU humanitarian	2018
		$614 million	US foreign aid	2016
		$924 million	USAID	2017
46.	Sudan	€41 million	EU humanitarian	2018
		$193 million	USAID	2017
47.	Swaziland	$59 million	USAID	2017
48.	Tanzania	$626 million	USAID	2017
49.	Togo	$7.4 million	USAID	2017
50.	Tunisia	$194 million	USAID	2017
51.	Uganda	€24 million	EU humanitarian	2018
		$741 million	USAID	2017
52.	Zambia	$419 million	USAID	2017
53.	Zimbabwe	$194 million	USAID	2017

Source: Waris and Waridah[389]

---

[389] This table is a compilation by Waris, A. and Waridah, M. (2019) of "Publicly available data on aid to African countries." Sources: Concern Worldwide (2018); European Commission (2013); Intelligent Economist (2018); New Internationalist (2018); and USAID (2018). The rate used is 1 EURO to 1.11 USD. ConverterX accessed 29 July 2019, www.currencyconverterx.com.

Printed in the United States
By Bookmasters